Patricia Wittberg, S.C.

Creating a Future for Religious Life

A SOCIOLOGICAL PERSPECTIVE

PAUL
New York

ACKNOWLEDGMENTS:
Paulist Press gratefully acknowledges use of: Quotation from *Complex Organizations* by Charles Perrow (McGraw-Hill, 1986) and *Becoming An Ex: The Process of Role Exit* by Helen Rose Fuchs Ebaugh (Chicago University Press, 1988) and from *Permanently Failing Organizations* by Marshall W. Meyer and Lynne G. Zucker, p. 23, © 1989 by Marshall W. Meyer and Lynne G. Zucker. Reprinted by permission of Sage Publications, Inc.

Library of Congress Cataloging-in-Publication Data

Wittberg, Patricia, 1947–
    Creating a future for religious life: a sociological perspective by Patricia Wittberg.
        p.   cm.
    Includes bibliographical references.
    ISBN 0-8091-3212-5
    1. Monasticism and religious orders.   2. Monastic and religious life.   3. Sociology, Christian (Catholic)   I. Title.
    BX2432.W46   1991
    255—dc20   90-48580
                                                                                  CIP

Published by Paulist Press
997 Macarthur Blvd.
Mahwah, N.J. 07430

Printed and bound in the United States of America

Contents

Dedication

To the present and future members of
Micah Intercommunity—

With God's help, a seed for the future.

Preface

No one warned me that writing a book is very much like having a baby—and not only in the superficial fact that its actual composition took me nine months. I also experienced the feeling that something was growing which had a life separate from my creating, and which was developing in ways I had not planned. Ideas would spring out at me from books I hadn't intended to read, worm themselves into my writing, and change the direction of whole chapters. Friends and acquaintances—some of whom I had not seen in years—would send me data they "thought I might be interested in." In the end I felt—as I imagine the parents of a newborn baby must feel—humble and awed, and very much aware that God had a larger hand in this project than I did.

Another similarity was the mounting urgency which seized the whole enterprise toward the end. It was almost as though the book intended to be born in April, whether I wanted it to or not. From January on, I neglected all sorts of other duties, including my search for a new fall teaching position. And, in the process, I received the aid of a large number of people who deserve more thanks than I can give here. Many persons read and gave me feedback on all or part of the manuscript: my professional colleagues Helen Rose Ebaugh, Michael Cuneo, Joe Fitzpatrick, S.J., and Esther Heffernan, O.P., as well as my sisters Joan Cook, S.C., Armin Cooper, S.C., Mary Ann Donovan, S.C., Margaret Ebbing, S.C., Mary Jo Gasdorf, S.C., Maureen Heverin, S.C., Glenda Reimer, S.C., and Montiel Rosenthal, S.C. I also had valuable input from women in other congregations: Joan Franks, O.P., Jeanne Hamilton, O.S.U., Edmund Harvey, R.S.H.M., Marie Celine Miranda, O.S.U., and Marilyn Sunderman, R.S.M. Jo-Ann Jakowski, C.S.S.F. furnished helpful statistics, and Mark Massa, S.J. was kind enough to connect me with Paulist Press. To all of these people, so generous with their time and concern, I owe a debt of gratitude. And although, like a new parent, I have trouble imagining that my "offspring" is anything less than perfect, I do realize that there are many faults—major and minor—in this book. For these I alone am responsible.

Finally, I owe profound thanks to the members of Micah Intercommunity, with whom I was privileged to live during my last two years in New York. Their love and acceptance, their joy and deep spirituality, supported me in more ways than I can name. To Barbara Lenniger, O.P., Veronica Miller, O.P., Bea McMahon, R.S.H.M., Katie Pierce, I.H.M., Carol Schommer, R.S.H.M., and Milagros Esteban, S.S.N.D., my thanks and my love.

Patricia Wittberg, S.C.
September 12, 1990

1

Introduction

Religious congregations are *social* groups. While this observation may seem self-evident, those who have written about religious life have rarely explored its implications. Surprisingly few systematic comparisons have been drawn, for example, between the dynamics of life in religious orders and those occurring in similarly constructed groups elsewhere. For the most part, religious life has been analyzed using only the concepts and analytical procedures of theology and—since Vatican II—of psychology. These disciplines have, of course, yielded profound insights which have benefited congregations as a whole as well as their individual members. For example, psychological research has been instrumental in developing an entirely new perspective on how the spiritual life is "enfleshed" in very human individuals who experience mid-life crises, emotionally fulfilling friendships, substance dependency, sexual generativity, depression and a host of other positive and negative psychic conditions as they move through life in their religious communities.

But religious men and women are not "pure spirits" socially any more than they are psychologically. As their individual psychological natures to some extent condition and give shape to their personal spiritual growth, so, too, the social dynamics in the groups of which they are members—in this case, their religious congregations—condition and shape the way in which they are able to live out their founders' charisms, to respond to (or even to hear) the Spirit's promptings in the world today, and, ultimately, to achieve and maintain the mental health which psychological research has found to be necessary to spiritual life. If a certain type of decision-making structure, a certain pattern of communication, or a particular manner of choosing group leaders has had specific, predictable effects in previously studied social groups, then we should be able to assume that, insofar as a religious congregation or a local house resembles these other groups, adoption of similar practices will result in similar outcomes. Of course, the religious charism of an order or the spiritual motivations of its members may enhance or mitigate the effects of their actions: no group of human beings is mechanically fated always to react in a certain way to a social stimulus. But the underlying tendency will still be there, and it would be advisable for the members and the leadership of a congregation to be aware of the potential outcomes which their decisions may have for their community. Such awareness may even be necessary for an order's survival in the present time of declining memberships and rising median ages.

This book will attempt to apply to religious congregations the sociological theories derived from research on other social groups. Its primary audience is intended to be members of religious communities. These members are facing serious survival decisions, the result of which will impact in predictable ways upon their group's functioning. To the extent that this audience recognizes aspects of their own communities in the pages that follow, I hope that they will be able to evaluate the likelihood of similar processes in their own congregation. Thus, they will become better equipped to choose and foster these processes if they are desirable, or to take steps to avoid them if they are not.

A secondary audience of this book is sociologists—especially those sociologists studying religion, formal organizations and women. If an awareness of sociological research could benefit the study—and the living—of religious life, the knowledge of how religious communities have handled issues such as structural change, member stratification and leadership selection could benefit the work of sociologists. Some religious communities have developed unique and novel solutions to the perennial problems any social group faces. To continue to ignore the ongoing dynamics of Roman Catholic religious congregations is to impoverish sociological analysis. A key contention of chapter 4, for example, will be that communities of nuns possess networks of empowering "weak ties" that far surpass the contacts available to other women. For the most part, feminist sociologists have been entirely unaware of this fact. Similarly, in all the sociological literature on intentional communities, there has been not one study of nuns (and only a few short articles on male orders)—even though they are the oldest and most successful examples of the intentional community model that exist. It is hoped that sociologists will be able to use some of the insights in this book as a basis for further research.

TYPES OF SOCIAL GROUPS

In sociological language, a "group" is any collection of more than three or four unrelated persons who interact together on a more or less permanent basis. These characteristics distinguish a group from a chance aggregation of persons in an elevator, although if the elevator breaks down between floors, the persons inside may become a temporary group as they work to free themselves. And if they are sufficiently indignant at the poor quality of elevator inspection in their city, they may form a permanent group to lobby for stricter code enforcement. Groups vary by size and by duration. Common goals also differentiate between groups: "instrumental groups," for example, have been formed to carry out a given task or set of tasks, while "expressive groups" gather to rejoice or grieve together. In addition to these dimensions, groups also vary by the amount of commitment which they require of their members. It is this last characteristic which will be discussed in the pages that follow.

Some groups, which we will call "associations" in this book, make comparatively few demands on those who would join them.

Members retain control over all aspects of their personal lives, and meet together periodically for purposes which can be either instrumental (Amnesty International, the American Psychological Association) or expressive (a Tuesday night bridge club, a local bowling league). Associations can, of course, be large or small, temporary or permanent, and it is not unusual for an individual to belong to several of them at once.

A second type, work groups, make more demands on their members than do associations. Individuals cede to their work group control over some aspects of their public lives, while remaining largely independent after the work day is over. In modern western societies, most workers are members of a specific type of large, formalized work group called a bureaucracy, in which the areas of group authority over the individual are carefully and meticulously codified. It is this bureaucratic work group which we will discuss here.

The type of group which makes the most extensive demands on its individual members is the intentional community. In such a group, the members cede control over some or all aspects of both their public (work) and private lives. The intentional community may therefore require its members to be celibate (or to be sexually promiscuous, or to marry a pre-selected mate), to live and work in a certain place (usually together), and to turn over all their personal earnings to a common fund. Throughout its history, the United States has been an especially fertile field for the development of a wide variety of both secular and religion-based intentional communities: in three hundred years there has never been a time when at least one such group did not exist here.[1] Some of these communities, such as the Oneida Community or the Shakers, were well known. Others were small and ephemeral. By 1965, there had already been over six hundred intentional communities started in the United States, and the years between 1965 and 1980 saw the establishment (and usually the demise) of twice as many more.[2]

In real life, most groups combine the characteristics of each of the three types of commitment. Several studies of large bureaucratic corporations have observed, for example, that the occupants of the highest rungs of General Motors or IBM must accept a good deal of corporate intrusion into their private lives.[3] Top executives may find that they are expected to be present at a wide variety of functions outside of stated business hours, to entertain in a certain way, or even to marry a certain kind of spouse and to send their children to certain kinds of schools. For top executives, therefore, the theoretically bureaucratic work group functions more as an intentional community.[4] Similarly, as associations or intentional communities become larger, their central cores often develop many bureaucratic tendencies. Several famous intentional communities—notably Amana and Oneida—have evolved into full-fledged corporate businesses in which no traces of their communitarian origins are left.

It is, actually, much more sociologically interesting to study these mixtures than it would be to investigate purely theoretical models of associations, bureaucracies and intentional communities. The ever-changing combination of commitment structures, communication patterns, decision-making procedures and other elements in mixed groups gives them unique strengths and vulnerabilities as they evolve from one form to another. Practices surviving from a previous time may result in inconsistent demands being placed on leaders or subordinates, thus possibly weakening a group's ability to govern its members at all. Alternatively, informal communication networks or residual loyalties inherited from some former organizational state may empower either the leadership or the rank and file in ways that are unusual compared to other groups. The task of the sociologist, in this instance, is to examine and describe the patterns of associational, bureaucratic and communitarian elements which are peculiar to a given group, so that its leadership and members may better decide how to strengthen their intra-organizational position vis-à-vis each other, and how best to relate to the group's surrounding environment.

RELIGIOUS CONGREGATIONS AS SOCIAL GROUPS

Before the Second Vatican Council, Roman Catholic religious congregations fell rather squarely into the intentional community category (although, as will be described below, they also had some bureaucratic aspects, especially during the 1950s). Since Vatican II, many communities have moved quite far from the intentional community model, adding an increasing number of bureaucratic and associational elements. Many communitarian elements have also been kept, however, and these do not always fit well with more recently adopted practices. A review of the sociological studies of other associations, bureaucracies and intentional communities may enable religious to be aware of and to evaluate the potential implications of their congregation's particular mix of these elements. What are the blind spots or weaknesses of a bureaucracy or an association as compared to an intentional community? In what tasks or activities do the other forms excel? What internal and external factors cause each type to grow or decline—and which of these factors are present in religious congregations today? What kind of new members can each type of group reasonably expect to attract? What aspects of a congregation—its associational, its bureaucratic, or its communitarian elements—should be emphasized in order to recruit those individuals who will be most suited to the type of organization toward which the order is evolving? What are the needs of the present members? What particular combination of elements could best meet these needs?

Previous sociological studies of these group types have rarely, if ever, been applied to religious life. In all the literature on intentional communities, for example, only one author discusses religious communities—in a chapter which focuses largely on the Jesuits.[5] No attempt has been made, even by feminist scholars, to consider congregations of women religious as intentional communities: for example, an issue of the women's studies journal *Signs* devoted entirely to women's communal living experiments makes no mention at all of nuns,[6] and several books on women's utopias are similarly lacking.[7] Likewise, sociological research on the dynamics of the Catholic Church as a bureaucratic organization has focused largely on the work satisfaction and recruitment of diocesan priests.[8] Of all this literature, only Ebaugh's *Out of the Cloister*[9] has ever addressed the organizational dilemmas faced by a religious congregation. Finally, as was mentioned in the preceding section, feminist writers and sociologists in general remain completely ignorant of the empowering associational characteristics of religious congregations of women, despite the fact that they constitute what is probably the oldest and most widespread women's network in the United States.[10]

Few sociological studies, therefore, have been done of religious congregations—either as associations, bureaucracies, or intentional communities. Decision-makers in religious communities who wished to benefit from sociological insights would have to make their own applications from the research done on other similar groups. However, as the president of the American Sociological Association has pointed out,[11] sociologists have been particularly remiss in disseminating the findings of their research to the public at large; there is, for example, no sociological equivalent to *Psychology Today*. Most religious orders are therefore unaware of the findings of sociological research which pertain to issues facing their orders. There is also a certain amount of resistance on the part of all religiously-based groups to admitting that they are subject to the same opportunities and stresses which affect secular human groups. So it is perhaps not surprising that religious orders show little realization of, or enthusiasm for, the contributions that sociology could make to their self-study.

This book is the study of one aspect of group organization —the type and extent of commitment which a group requires of its members—and it will attempt to apply some of the concepts and hypotheses thus developed to religious congregations. In the process, I hope that it will also serve as a first step toward an integration of sociology and the spiritual life, comparable to the cross-fertilization that has already taken place between psychology and spirituality. It is impossible today to open a volume of

Review for Religious, or any other comparable magazine covering religious life, without finding at least one article devoted to some psychological topic: stress and burnout among ministers, for example, or the necessity of a positive self-image for spiritual growth. Workshops, retreats and entire graduate degree programs have been developed, for example, to encourage the use of Myers-Briggs profiles or Intensive Journaling in spiritual direction, or to apply the psychology of aging to elderly religious. Similarly, perhaps someday there will be journals and workshops devoted to the socially integrating effects of ritual in a group, or to the limits upon decision-making that result when an organization's entire leadership is drawn from similar intra- or extra-organizational backgrounds. Such congregation-level crises as rapid membership expansion (or decline), the death of the original founder, or the attenuation of group commitment with increasing geographic dispersal could also be studied in this way.

Religious life is clearly experiencing a difficult period. One of Gerald Arbuckle's recent books, for example, begins with the blunt paragraph:

> Many religious congregations today are in chaos. They are not sure about the meaning, contemporary relevance, or mission of religious life and, on the practical level, they find it difficult to cope with often rapidly declining numbers, few or no vocations and the rising average ages of membership.[12]

Such systemic disarray cannot be addressed simply by trying to alleviate the psychological distress which it causes in individuals, as necessary as this may be. The dynamics of the entire process of organizational adaptation and change as a religious congregation moves from one form of commitment to another must also be understood.

One final comment. The sociological perspective is only one of the many possible perspectives that could be used to analyze religious life. Each discipline's concepts and analytical procedures lead its followers to focus on a given set of topics and relationships and to neglect others—much like the fable of the blind men and the elephant. If a finding or a recommendation presented in this book contradicts the findings of psychology or theology about religious life, this does not mean that the conclusions of the latter disciplines are wrong. They are simply partial conclusions —as are those of sociology. A balance of these partial visions is necessary. It will be a central argument of chapter 2 of this book, for example, that one of the reasons some religious communities are declining is because they have neglected some of the basic socially-integrating mechanisms which are needed to keep their group together, and have concentrated instead on addressing the individual psychological needs of their members. Other communities grow because they have somehow stumbled upon these social integration mechanisms, even though this may be at the expense of the theological or psychological aspects of religious life. In order both to grow and to meet the spiritual and psychological needs of its members, a community would need to draw upon the findings of all three disciplines. Another distracting element may be the discovery that (e.g.) celibacy is required in religious life at least partly because it serves a concrete sociological purpose in all intentional communities. This, however, does not detract from the theological purposes which celibacy also serves. As Bennett Berger remarks in his study of counter-cultural communes, it may be better for a group in the long run if its moral and ideological beliefs are reinforced by a certain degree of self- or group-interest: one should avoid "the ascetic notion that the harder it is to sustain one's moral beliefs, the more profound becomes one's moral achievement."[13] To revert again to what will be a central theme of this book, it is probably impossible for any group of human beings to maintain its ideological commitment without at least some grounding of this commitment in the group's social practices.

It may also bother some readers to see religious communities analyzed clinically, as if they were no different from the March of Dimes, IBM, or the Hare Krishnas. This may be because readers mistakenly confuse "is" with "ought" when reading studies of religious life, and assume that the author is recommending or approving a tendency which he or she is merely describing.[14] My own belief is that just as the personal incarnation of Jesus in a human nature accepted and affirmed even the physical and psychological limitations of that nature in its quest for spiritual growth, so the social incarnation of Jesus in his church (what we used to call the mystical body) also accepts and affirms the limitations inherent in the group nature of the people of God. If it is a delusion, and ultimately self-defeating, for an individual to attempt to achieve psychological perfection (and even worse to believe that one has already achieved it), so, too, is it similarly delusive to believe that one's group can ever completely free itself from the fetters of its inherent limitations. The important thing is for a community to be aware of and to accept these limitations, and to take them into account as they plan and work to follow the voice of the Spirit into the twenty-first century.

2

Intentional Communities
and Religious Life

A Definition of Intentional Communities

Throughout history, most religious congregations have been intentional communities, and the majority continue to retain many characteristics of this most demanding of all group forms. There have been various sociological definitions of the term "intentional community," which I have summarized elsewhere as "a group of persons living together on a more or less permanent basis, who voluntarily surrender control over some choices which are normally considered private for the sake of establishing a whole new way of life."[1] In an intentional community, therefore, the group's transcendent mission or goal takes precedence over the needs of the individual members. The members voluntarily give the community (or its leaders) the right to decide what work they will do, whether (and whom) they will marry, where they will live, and even what they will do with their "free" time. Income is turned over to a common fund and the members usually have little discretionary money of their own. In return, the community takes care of the individual both emotionally and financially, and offers him/her the privilege of participating in a common endeavor which is believed to be of supreme worth and importance.

In its most typical form, an intentional community is also a total institution, which means that the members live, work and recreate together, having very little contact with persons or ideas from the "outside world."[2] This deliberate isolation is especially necessary to the extent that the community's way of life is based on values or beliefs which are different from the mainstream of the society in which they are located. Without the support and protection which a total institution's isolation provides, the members of an intentional community are in danger of having their motivation eroded by the competing values of the surrounding culture.

Many people, especially religious who may have had negative experiences of being oppressed or limited by the kinds of demands which an intentional community can make on them, may wonder how a mature adult could ever join such a group. Indeed, distraught parents whose sons or daughters have joined modern-day cults have often resorted to hiring deprogrammers to kidnap them away from such a destructive environment. Relatives and friends usually feel that cult members must have been "brainwashed" by their evil leader, since they could not possibly have submitted to such discipline of their own free will. This opposition parallels the distress and anger which some families used to express when one of their children entered religious life; older members in some congregations still remember stories of fellow religious who had to defy intense parental pressure in order "to respond to God's call."[3] In every age, outsiders have found the dedication and self-sacrifice of intentional community members hard to understand.

Despite their often de-individualizing demands, however, intentional communities continue to exert a profound attraction for many people, an attraction based on the idealism of sacrificing oneself for a noble cause in the supportive presence of others who share the same vision. "Human nature is not something existing separately in the individual . . . one is never more human, *and as a rule never happier,* than when he is sacrificing his narrow and merely private interests to the higher call of the congenial group."[4] [italics mine] As he interviewed apostates from the Bruderhof, a twentieth century Hutterite community which still exists in upstate New York, Benjamin Zablocki noted the intense longing which many of them felt for the community they had left, even as they expressed the belief that they were healthier and freer away from it:

> A number of apostates confessed that they were afraid to go back to the Bruderhof, even for a short visit. They were afraid that a whiff of [the Bruderhof members'] joy would draw them back into the fold again, despite their firm resolutions to the contrary. A majority of the others with whom I had contact exhibited manifestations of what has come to be known among them as "exile syndrome," a dispirited, purposeless drifting, viewing any possible life outside the Bruderhof as dull, pale and meaningless. Exile syndrome generally wears off after a year or so, but in some it has persisted more than five years. It might almost be said that Bruderhof joy is habit-forming.[5]

This tension between individual autonomy and the desire to belong to an intimate communal group is endemic in modern western society. Perhaps America's stress on "rugged individualism" —so well documented in popular books like *Habits of the Heart*[6]—is the reason why intentional communities have also flourished here. Our culture's strong and habitual emphasis on freedom and autonomy may precipitate a reactive flight by some individuals to the security of the opposite extreme.

COMMITMENT IN INTENTIONAL COMMUNITIES

The fact remains that intentional communities do make intense demands on their members, demands which, ordinarily, would be considered infringements on their individual rights. This is so because, in order to survive, an intentional community must accomplish two tasks.[7] First of all, it must ensure that the work(s) it has defined as essential to its survival are carried out.

Money necessary for food and shelter must be earned, meals must be cooked, living areas must be cleaned, and group decisions must be made, whether or not an individual member would prefer things to be done differently in a particular instance. Secondly, the intentional community must sufficiently satisfy the needs of its members that they will not become fed up and leave, and it must attract enough new members to compensate for apostates and for deaths. Obviously, these two tasks can be contradictory: to the extent that members are dissatisfied with their group-assigned tasks or with a given group decision, they will have at least some incentive to leave. It is often the most seemingly insignificant aspects of daily communal life that grate the most severely on members—the tendency of X to leave her dirty coffee cup in the sink, for example, or Y's failure to clean away his bathtub ring. To counterbalance the centrifugal forces of individual needs and preferences that tend to drive its members apart, an intentional community needs to create and maintain a strong sense of corporate commitment that will draw them together.

Commitment to a Charismatic Leader

The first way to unite an intentional community is through a strong charismatic leader, usually the founder, who can require obedience by the mere force of his/her personality, holiness, or other compelling characteristics.[8] Such a leader is crucial for inspiring lifetime commitment in the other members of an intentional community, for "unless there is strong, unhesitating leadership . . . American individualist antinomianism soon begins to tear things asunder."[9] The actual teachings of charismatic leaders are often not as important as the sheer force of their personalities and example. They have a special talent for dramatizing and articulating the common vision that unites their followers, thus inspiring in the entire community a devotion and a sense of mission that can withstand great odds.[10]

The problem is that charismatic leadership cannot last; it is inevitably "routinized," as Weber puts it, either upon the death of the founder, or when the group gets too large to be in effective contact with his or her charisma. Even before the founder dies or the group's size increases, its earliest fervor may die down considerably; it is difficult to sustain "white hot mobilization" indefinitely.[11] Charismatic leaders from Moses to Mao Tse-tung have bemoaned the straying of their followers from their initial enthusiasm. As the disaster of China's Cultural Revolution shows, however, attempts by charismatic leaders to rekindle the original devotion to their leadership often backfire. Leaders can lose their charisma and fall from grace if they disrupt the delicate balance between the active *exercise* of leadership power by the top and the active *granting* of leadership authority by the bottom: "Followers are predisposed to receive and act only on certain messages."[12] If commune leaders always demand more sacrifices of their followers and purge any who seem too lukewarm, they risk disaffection and rebellion.[13]

Other Forms of Commitment

No intentional community can thus rely very long on charismatic leadership for its primary source of group loyalty. Those communities that survive must transfer their members' commitment from the charismatic leader to the ideals which he or she represented. This ideological commitment is "the central fact of all intentional communities," without which they cannot maintain the necessary spirit of self-sacrifice in their members.[14] Ideological commitment, however, is in constant danger of being eroded by the values and beliefs of the surrounding society. Therefore, two other types of commitment are often used to bolster the effects of ideological commitment: "cognitive" or "utilitarian" commitment, by which members weigh the benefits they gain by membership against the benefits they could gain elsewhere, and "cathetic" or "emotional" commitment, which expresses the bonds of friendship and familial attachment. Cathetic commitment, in fact, is the "most powerful single predictor" of whether an individual will stay in or leave an intentional community.[15] "No one stays in an intentional community because of ideology; the ideology will only be adhered to if the community gives one a feeling of home. Conversely, the stresses of living in a community would be intolerable if there were no ideological backing to one's life in it."[16]

In addition to faith in a common ideology, therefore, members of an intentional community also need the bonds of common friendship within the group, as well as a belief that they are gaining certain concrete and practical benefits from their membership. Only thus will they be willing to sacrifice, over an extended period of time, their individual interests and opinions for the sake of the group. If this consensus ever breaks down, the members experience increasing alienation.[17] Alienation varies in severity. Members may disagree, first of all, over strategies to gain agreed-upon goals: Should one seek enlightenment through this or that form of meditation? Does harmony with nature require vegetarianism? On a deeper level, members may dispute which of several group goals or activities should receive priority: the communal farm or the arts and crafts shop? sanctification of self or evangelization? The most profound degree of alienation is when members disagree over the existence, relevance, or value of a goal which the intentional community's ideology had named as primary: Is celibacy psychologically healthy? Is common life possible or desirable? Whatever its degree, however, any sort of alienation is dangerous to the cohesion and the very survival of an intentional community.

COMMITMENT-FOSTERING MECHANISMS

To avoid alienation, an intentional community must maintain its members' ideological, cathetic and utilitarian commitment even after its initial charismatic leadership has been "routinized" and the inspiring presence of its founder is no longer available. Communities which survive do so by adopting several common mechanisms which foster and protect their members' commitment. "To have a conversion experience is nothing much. The real thing is to be able to keep on taking it seriously; to retain the sense of its plausibility. This is where the religious community comes in; it provides the indispensable plausibility structure for the new reality."[18]

In reading about these universal commitment mechanisms, which have been independently rediscovered time and again by intentional communities, the reader will probably be struck by how much they resemble practices common in pre-Vatican II religious life. This is to be expected. Religious congregations, especially before Vatican II, *were* intentional communities, and those that survived did so because they employed, as all successful intentional communities have had to employ, techniques such as these to maintain their members' commitment.

Common Ritual and Traditions

In order to safeguard its ideological and cathetic commitment, it is important that an intentional community enact this commitment frequently in common ritual celebrations. "These rituals both express and reinforce jointly-held values, and represent ways of coming together as a group, of feeling closer to one another. For this reason, group rituals are often the most significant and important aspect of community life to members, for it is here that the higher, transcendent meaning of living in utopia is affirmed."[19] Successful communes devote extensive proportions of their members' time to ritual and traditions, which may be as solemn and sacred as a formal Easter vigil service or as simple and everyday as holding hands and singing before meals. The more these rituals and traditions permeate daily life, the more they will reinforce the beliefs and values that give meaning and purpose to the group's existence.

> All important occasions in the Bruderhof are marked by a love meal. . . . The dining room tables are arranged in a horseshoe, spread with white tablecloths and specially decorated; the dining room is lit by candles. . . . Everyone gathers outside

before the meal. They sing songs and walk into the room together.[20]

Ritual times are, by their very nature, times of coming together, and the close family-feeling instilled by the rituals is often the aspect most attractive to the participants.

Working, Living and Playing Together

At the beginning of this chapter, it was mentioned that intentional communities are often "total institutions," that is, their members live, work, and spend all or most of their recreational time together. This togetherness is another commitment mechanism, designed to foster and increase both ideological and cathetic commitment. Ties within the community must become stronger than those outside; previous attachment to nonmember family and friends must be broken. Family terminology such as "Brother" or "Sister" is often adopted for fellow members, indicating that the intentional community has become one's true family.[21]

Within the community, particularistic attachments must not be allowed to disrupt the bond which a member feels to the larger group. Researchers of intentional communities are unanimous in stating that monogamous marriage, for example, is a threat to community. Successful communes have, therefore, usually mandated either celibacy or promiscuity (the Oneida Community's complex marriage is an example of the latter). Even in those cases where commune members are allowed to marry, members' mates may be pre-selected for them, or their marriage may be ritually subordinated to the group. "Strong institutions [intentional communities] should develop policies hostile to members forming extraordinarily close relationships. The small group or clique loyalties developed in such relationships may be inconsistent with the principle of obedience and with group coherence."[22]

Common work and recreational activities foster the group's familial bond, as does eating the main meal, or all the meals, together. Members are also allowed little time alone; their days are usually structured so that little free time remains to them.[23] The constant presence of others who share one's beliefs and value system, and the lack of time for reflection alone, act to reinforce the members' ideological commitment as well as their attachment to each other.

As numbers increase, the intentional community must take special steps to maintain this familial intimacy. Some Canadian Hutterite groups, for example, divide in two whenever the original community exceeds a set number; the groups draw lots to determine which half will move elsewhere.[24] If an intentional community remains united but lives in different locations, members may be required to switch frequently between living groups, in order to attenuate attraction to a particular sub-group and increase loyalty to the whole. Through such practices, the members not only develop strong cathetic bonds of attachment to the group at large, but also are constantly surrounded by persons who believe and value the same motivating ideology that they themselves espouse.

Boundary Maintenance

The essential complement of familial togetherness as a commitment mechanism is boundary maintenance. It is very important for members to be aware that a strong division exists between insiders and outsiders. Movement across the boundary of the group is regulated; members rarely leave, and the presence and participation of outsiders is severely restricted.[25] Isolation from contaminating outsider ideas must also be enforced in order to protect the unifying ideology from competition.

> Great care is taken to see to it that the children never hear visitors, delivery men, or other outsiders say a dirty word. Play with neighborhood children is discouraged. The adult members seldom retain membership in any outside organization, and at one time even their mail was censored and their newspapers and magazines were checked for objectionable material which was clipped out.[26]

Another protective device is to forbid members to attend, or to allow their children to attend, secular or worldly schools. The Amish, while not an intentional community in the strict sense, have utilized separate schools to protect their children from mainstream American culture.

In addition to protecting ideological commitment, boundary maintenance also fosters cathetic commitment by increasing a feeling of group identity. Sometimes this is reinforced by the wearing of similar clothes. A recent study of a strict Mennonite sect reported that as long as the group was relatively isolated on the American frontier, "clothing was not a major issue."[27] Only when their physical isolation came to an end in the twentieth century, and there was danger of being absorbed by the larger culture, was a formal dress code prescribed. Rigidity of adherence to a dress code also serves to "place" a member in a spiritual hierarchy, and to symbolize his or her internalization of the values of the group. Conversely, by uniting together against deviant members who do not so conform, the observant members reinforce their feelings of group identity and delimit the bounds of acceptable conduct.[28]

Sacrifice

Paradoxically, the act of requiring members to give up something can also be a mechanism to increase their commitment to the group. Several writers have pointed out that an unpleasant mental conflict would be created if one believed that the cause for which one was sacrificing so much was, in reality, worthless. Individuals avoid this "cognitive dissonance"[29] by convincing themselves that their cause really is noble and just. In fact, the more one has given up for it, the more sacred and valuable the goal may become.

In addition to strengthening ideological commitment, communal renunciation can also strengthen group solidarity:

> That was one of my troubles, giving up clothing. Certain skirts. One velvet skirt I had [laughing]. Oh, how I loved that velvet skirt! [Q. Why did you have to give it up?] Well . . . we

were made to feel ... that you shouldn't want something particularly pretty and that looked well on you, that compliments you. This was pride. ... Well, I remember I struggled with this and finally one day I was able to march over with a few of these things and my velvet skirt. And I just felt, when I expressed this to [the housemothers] *they rejoiced with me.*[30] [italics mine]

Utilitarian commitment is also enhanced by sacrifice; if a member has surrendered all of his or her property to the group, the fear of impoverishment may be sufficient to discourage leaving.

The balance between sacrifice and group loyalty is sometimes difficult to maintain. If the daily demand for sacrifice becomes excessive, members will leave, and it is often unclear exactly where this "breaking point" will be. If high initiation costs (celibacy, for example, or the surrender of all one's property) were required in order to enter the group, members will be less likely to question the daily demands which are made upon them and, initially at least, will be less likely to leave. Decreasing the likelihood of exit is another reason, besides its beneficial cathetic effects on group togetherness, why celibacy is often required as an initiation cost in intentional communities. But once the members' questioning starts, it quickly becomes intense.[31] Members in such situations may actually exit sooner than if no initiation costs had been demanded.

Mortification

An extremely powerful commitment mechanism is the utilization of several practices whereby the individual "dies" to his/her defective, individual self in order to be reborn into a new, better identity conferred by the group. Many intentional communities employ self-criticism sessions similar to the Chapter of Faults in pre-Vatican II religious congregations. The establishment of a feeling of guilt and worthlessness is a prelude to adopting the community's point of view: "Gradually, a voice within them was made to say, ever more loudly: 'It is my sinfulness, and not their injustice, which causes me to suffer.' "[32] This self-stripping is especially effective if, after the group spends some time reducing the individual's sense of self-worth, he or she is reaffirmed through membership in the community:

> Suddenly and unexpectedly, a door opens for the novice. He is offered a choice: 'There are two ways for you to go: one way leads to life, and the other to death. If you want the road that leads to life, you must take our way.'[33]

The member who accepts the "road to life" is, by that acceptance alone, admitted to an elite which has chosen a better, purer way. Often a new name will be conferred as a symbol of this rebirth,[34] or the entrants may shed their clothes in a formalized ritual and assume new (usually uniform) garb as a symbol of this changed identity: "Strip me, O Lord, of my former self, with its evil deeds and ways, and clothe me with a new nature which has been created after the model of Jesus Christ, in justice and holiness and truth."[35] If effectively done, mortification is a powerful commitment tool, for the member's whole self-esteem comes to depend on his/her membership in good standing within the group.

LIABILITIES OF INTENTIONAL COMMUNITY COMMITMENT MECHANISMS

Readers of the above description of commitment mechanisms in intentional communities ought by this time to have realized some of the basic liabilities of these techniques. The first and most obvious is that such practices can be quite destructive psychologically: "All monastic communities, no matter how enduring, pay a severe price in psychological terms for their success."[36] At its worst, the strain of subordinating one's identity to the group can become pathological (the Manson family and Jonestown are examples), but even comparatively humane and "respectable" groups such as the Hutterites have a high rate of colitis and many members regularly use tranquilizers such as Valium.[37]

The forced homogeneity of intentional communities means either that intense, ego-destroying pressures must be used to resocialize members, or else that members must be recruited at younger and more psychologically plastic ages. The normal maturation process to psychological adulthood may become thwarted in very young recruits to an intentional community.

The commitment mechanisms also foster organizational rigidity and resistance to change. Because so much depends upon the unvaried performance of a ritual, or on wearing a particular style of clothes, the community may be reluctant to change even the most seemingly trivial practices. If the intentional community is also a total institution, its isolation will render the members less aware of changes in their surrounding environment. In the long run, this rigidity may prove harmful for the community's survival. The Shakers, for example, drew many of their converts from the orphan children for whom they cared, and from widowed or abandoned women with no other means of support. With the coming of twentieth century welfare systems, and with longer average parental life spans (which means that fewer orphans are available), their major recruitment sources dried up. Few Shakers now remain, and fewer join them.

A final disadvantage of an intentional community's commitment mechanisms is that they can easily usurp ideological commitment to the founder's original vision and thus decrease the fervor which this vision had instilled in the first generation of members. Increasingly, members will remain because of cathetic and utilitarian ties only. Zablocki notes that Bruderhof members who may have wished to leave were often reluctant to do so, since they had surrendered all their material goods upon entering and had no idea how they would make a living "outside." Also, leaving was difficult for cathetic reasons: "All the people who matter to you will be cut off from you forever. A member is often not sure if his own spouse will come with him."[38] In such an atmosphere, it is inevitable that the original level of ideological fervor and commitment will decline in the face of more mundane concerns, even though a majority of the members remain. Then, when outside changes threaten the community, the members may have few deeply-rooted commitment resources available to resist them.

Intentional communities, therefore, alternate between two poles of commitment and alienation, founding fervor and dissolution. To the extent that they adopt commitment mechanisms to protect their original vision, the members will be vulnerable to having that vision usurped by the very practices that were designed to safeguard it. Also, the increasing rigidity and enforced homogeneity that accompany successful commitment mechanisms will gradually lead to the group's becoming "out of sync" with its environment. The community may not be able to change rapidly enough to meet the new conditions, and its members' ideological commitment may no longer be deep enough to sustain them even if such changes do occur in their group. On the other hand, if commitment-enhancing mechanisms are *not* adopted, or if they are later discarded, the intentional community will no longer be able to require from its members the sacrifices it needs for survival. Intentional communities usually do not last very long—most flourish and dissolve within a single generation.[39] And yet the original thirst for belonging to a group which is committed to a transcendent ideal does not die, and new communities constantly spring up to replace the old.

Life Cycles in Religious Communities

The dynamics inherent in the tension between commitment and alienation, the need for community and for individual autonomy, can be used to shed light on the cycles which several authors have observed occurring in religious congregations.[40] A recurring pattern of foundation, expansion, stabilization, and breakdown has developed time and again throughout the history of western Christianity, in intevals of two hundred and fifty to three hundred and fifty years. During a "critical period" at the end of each cycle, most religious congregations (Cada estimates between sixty-five and seventy-five percent) die out. The remainder are "refounded"[41] and begin the cycle anew. Previous studies have described this pattern without explaining the causal forces behind it. In the following section of this chapter, I will use the dynamics that have been discovered in studies of other intentional communities in order to explore what these causal forces might be.

A SHORT HISTORY OF THE LIFE CYCLES OF RELIGIOUS CONGREGATIONS

According to Cada, the first age of organized religious life in Christianity lasted from 200 until 500 A.D. This was the "Age of the Desert," in which wilderness areas were seen as the last refuge of the devil. (Indeed, our word "pagan" is an echo of a time when Christianity was primarily an urban religion—"paganus" originally meant "country dweller.") Religious life during this period was seen as an intense *solitary* combat with the forces of darkness. Desert Fathers and Mothers would undertake heroic acts of self-denial and penance as a substitute for martyrdom and as a means of winning the devil's realm for Christ.

By the fifth century, a combination of abuses within the desert brand of religious life and the outside changes brought on by the barbarian invasions of western Europe led to the Age of Monasticism. This second type of organized religious life lasted from 500 until about 1200 A.D., with a refounding period (the Cluniac and Cistercian reforms) occurring at approximately the millennium. Religious life during this period was defined as life in a monastery under the discipline of a Holy Rule. Obeying the Rule's strictures (which were generally much less demanding than the "excessive" penances of the desert-era religious) was the primary means of achieving the goal of monastic religious life: to praise God and to unite oneself with Christ. In the "Dark Ages" following the fall of the Roman empire, monasteries served as islands of learning and safety.

With the revitalization of towns and commerce following the crusades, the rural life of the monastic religious became less suited to the needs and temper of the church. A third age, the Age of the Mendicant Orders, began, and lasted from 1200 until 1500 A.D. Under this new model, religious life was exemplified by the simple friar who begged for his[42] keep as he followed in the footsteps of Jesus—giving all of his worldly goods to the poor and preaching the love of Christ wherever he went. The Age of Mendicant Orders ended with the Protestant reformation when, once again, new challenges arose which called for a new response. In the Age of Apostolic Orders (1500–1800), religious came to be considered as an elite corps of devoted servants, ready to aid the church in areas of special need. A high level of personal holiness and education was demanded, since members were often sent to isolated places where they could not live in community. A long formation period and intense spiritual direction helped to achieve this commitment.

The fifth age of organized religious life, according to Cada's summary, was the Age of Teaching Congregations. Lasting from the early 1800s until the present day, this model defines religious life as dedicating one's life to saving one's own soul and serving others. Personal holiness was sought in the company of a group of like-minded individuals, who simultaneously devoted themselves to some specific ministry such as education, health care, or social work. It is this fifth age, Cada and Hostie felt, that is currently approaching its cyclical stage of decline, dissolution and (possibly) rebirth.

Common Patterns

Cada and Hostie observed several common patterns in each historical cycle. Initially, each new model was not perceived as *really* being "religious life." The Benedictines did no intensive works of penance; the Franciscans did not live in monasteries. Despite official reservations about their authenticity, however, each new form enjoyed tremendous initial success, because, as Hostie remarked, the new model was more in tune with "a vast field of force"—it answered the needs of the times in a way that the old order, rigidly bound to now-obsolete practices, could not.[43] Within decades of their founding, the new orders attracted large numbers of adherents: the Franciscans gained five thousand members in their first ten years, the Dominicans thirteen thousand in less than four decades.[44] In the most recent era of teaching congregations, between 1815 and 1965, twice as many religious communities were founded as in any period of similar length.[45] The success which the new communities had in attracting members eventually won over the authorities as well as the Catholic laity, and the new model came to be considered a bona fide form of religious life.

Another perduring historical pattern was that, in all but the Mendicant period, at least twice as many women as men entered religious life.[46] However, the women's congregations were usually founded by men, and men provided the models upon which they were based, even when a woman founder tried to avoid such influence.[47] Men also did most of the writing about religious life, and naturally tended to concentrate on the male orders they knew best. Thus, the casual student of the history of religious life might be led to the erroneous conclusion that members of religious orders were predominantly male.

The founders of successful religious congregations usually displayed a unique combination of charismatic attractiveness and practical ability, and they wrote the constitutions codifying their founding vision only after ten or twenty years' experience.[48] Often a founder would go through a sort of "apprenticeship" of several failed attempts to establish a religious congregation before he or she hit on the right combination of characteristics to meet the needs of the new era.[49] Women founders usually fell into one of two types: the "strong," who attempted to establish communities after their own visions, and the "devout," who were recruited by a male (usually a cleric) to begin a sister community to the order the man had founded.[50]

As several writers have observed, congregations of women were usually forced to adopt the monastic, cloistered model of religious life, whether or not this model was congruent with their founder's original vision.[51] Otherwise, as was the case with the Beguines in medieval Europe, they were forced to disband. Hostie cites the example of Angela Merici, who founded the Ursulines in 1535 at the age of sixty. Although St. Angela had deliberately specified that her followers were to take no vows, wear no habit, and observe no cloister or common life, her community was re-conformed to the traditional model after her death. Under Charles Borromeo, the three simple vows were imposed in 1572, and the wearing of a habit in 1579. By 1612, many of the Ursulines were enclosed and taking solemn vows.[52] It is doubtful if Angela Merici would have recognized the community she had founded.

The writers who have observed the "remonasticizing" of the various cycles of women's religious communities have usually treated of this phenomenon as an example of the church's suspicion of women's sexuality, and of the need to keep women "in their place" and subordinate to the male hierarchy. This is undoubtedly true, to some extent. But it ignores two key facts. First, the women themselves often requested this transformation. Second, male orders also gradually "lapsed" back to a more monastic model, even if this was not rigidly imposed upon them from the outside as it had been for the women:

> St. Dominic founded the Order for preaching, a role previously restricted only to bishops. Dominic wanted all aspects of Dominican life to support this preaching mission, and moved his friars out of monasteries and into "convents," where they would come together after having been out preaching. Observances, such as those in monasteries . . . were not important to him if they did not support the life of preaching. Yet in every reform of the Order since Dominic's death in 1221, monastic observances rather than the preaching of the friars have been stressed.[53]

COMMITMENT MECHANISMS AND THE CYCLES OF RELIGIOUS LIFE

The Routinization of Religious Charisma

What social forces, then, are behind the recurring transformation of new models of religious life back to some version of the monastic model? One factor appears to be the persistence of the older model in the minds of the hierarchy who certified the new congregations, the members who joined them, and the laity who interacted with them. As Hostie put it, "The initiatives, however revolutionary, of Angela Merici and her subsequent avatars illustrate how strong and tenacious the traditional formulas are in the evolution of religious life. As soon as the foundation expands, it is made to conform to the expectations and the imperatives of the prevailing mind set. But let us be fair. Certainly their protectors and promoters, Charles Borromeo especially, imposed it on them. But it is no less true that the members who came aspired to this model and worked toward it with all their energy. *One would even say that such a spectacular expansion could not have been realized without this reversal of perspective.*"[54] [italics mine] In order to be taken seriously and respected by the general public, as well as to obtain the official certification necessary to operate within the Catholic Church, members of new-model congregations felt the necessity of conforming, at least to some extent, to the tried and true model.[55] Perduring over the seven hundred years between 500 and 1200, the monastic model had become an objective reality in itself, shaping the way that all the people touched by western culture defined "true" religious life.[56]

But there is another reason why the expansion and growth of religious communities—whatever their original model—could not have happened without the adoption of at least some monastic characteristics. *The monastic model successfully provided the commitment mechanisms necessary for the survival of religious congregations after the death of their charismatic founder.* The founder's vision usually made extensive demands on his/her followers. The only way these demands could be sustained after the founder's death was if they were periodically reaffirmed through ritual, safeguarded from contamination by outside ideologies, and made valuable through continued sacrifice. Zablocki notes that, after their initial fervor wanes, intentional communities have only two options: to transform their charismatic stage into a stable system in which ideological commitment is reinforced by cathetic and utilitarian commitment, or else to become looser associations which make fewer demands on their members. "Members of an association regain virtually full personal autonomy, and the commune becomes a co-operative venture in support of its members' self-interests. Many of these latter types last two or three decades, *but rarely are they able to produce a second generation.*"[57] [italics mine] Historically, therefore, religious congregations which failed to adopt intentional community commitment mechanisms also failed to survive. And the monastic model, with its successful commitment mechanisms, was readily available (for women, even mandated) as an accepted framework to which the new community's organization, however much it may have originally differed, could be adapted. Once a congregation adopted monastic commitment mechanisms, the solidification and institutionalization of their ideological commitment also led, albeit gradually, to a decline in fervor and a rise in other, "lesser" motivations.

The Decline of Religious Congregations

At the end of each cycle of religious life, the established communities entered upon a period of stagnation and decline. The stabilizing commitment mechanisms which had ensured their original survival after their founder's death also led to an increasing disjuncture between the practices of the communities and the needs of the church and its members. This disjuncture took place at varying rates, depending on the focus of the congregation and on the rapidity of change in the surrounding culture. Hostie notes that orders founded around a specific work were vulnerable to sudden declines if the need for that work was suddenly removed. The Knights Templar, for example, ceased functioning as a religious congregation after the necessity of guarding pilgrims to the Holy Land disappeared.[58] The most recent age, that of the Teaching Congregations, also seems to be coming to an end more quickly than former periods, as the ever-accelerating changes of the post-industrial era render less pressing some of the needs which these congregations had been founded to meet, and as expanding career opportunities for the second and third generations of the immigrants' children render other lifestyles more feasible and more attractive than religious life.

In addition to rendering congregations more and more "out of sync" with their surrounding environments, the religious communities' commitment mechanisms also weakened the force of their original founding ideology/world view and substituted other forms of commitment. Arbuckle speaks of "myth drift" as congregations accommodate to secular values and their original counter-cultural ideology begins to lose its force.[59] If the members are held in the community largely by cathetic and utilitarian bonds (and if, as society changes, the utilitarian advantages become less and less pronounced), they are more vulnerable to various types of alienation. Disagreements arise, at first over strategies or ministerial works, later over the very founding myth itself. Plagued by increasing irrelevance without and dissension within, the congregation slides toward decline. Fewer and fewer new members are recruited, and many already-professed members leave.

Unless an order is actively suppressed, however, the dying of a congregation is a slow process. "Organizations rarely die gracefully. There is too much invested in their immortality for people to let go without conflict or tension, or for leaders to be perfectly honest about the possibility of system death."[60] The membership and the leaders may deny that decline is, in fact, taking place, and resist efforts to conform their community to the characteristics of any new model which may be developing.

The Perils of Refounding

While most congregations eventually die out, a minority do manage to emerge from their period of decline reinvigorated and adapted to the demands of the new era. Cada, Arbuckle and other writers have termed this phenomenon "refounding." It is important to emphasize, however, that *all* major refoundings are fraught with schism and controversy. "Everywhere the reform [of the Franciscans] unleashed violent internal opposition. The movement . . . split the entire group in two."[61] There are basic socio-

logical reasons why many members of a religious community
might consider the "cure" of refounding to be worse than the
"disease" of declining membership. By definition, "refounding"
means returning to the original charism of the founder, updated to
meet the needs of the present society, perhaps, but still as ideolo-
gically demanding as the original charism had been. However,
many members of the declining congregation no longer possess
this ideological commitment, or they may have adapted their ideological beliefs in several different ways to the mainstream secular
culture and now be of varying minds as to which is the authorita-
tive version. They may be bound to the congregation by cathetic
and utilitarian bonds alone, or they may even be held only by
looser, associational ties, while the major foci for their life and
work lie elsewhere. To reawaken a unified ideological commitment in such a diverse group, refounding persons often have to be
charismatic leaders in their own right (Teresa of Avila would be
an example). *It must never be forgotten that charismatic leaders are
potentially dangerous.* They do not appeal to their followers' rationality, but rather to their devotion and personal loyalty. And
history is full of charismatic leaders who have abused their power.
"The problem is that charismatic leaders, due to the emotional
tone they possess and project, are quite capable of leading groups
into disorder and encouraging undesirable forms of anxiety re-
lease. Thus, Adolf Hitler, a charismatic leader, persuaded the
German people to transform their mild anti-Semitism into brutal
genocide. And the American examples of the Reverend Jim Jones
and Charles Manson also come to mind."[62] Less ideologically-
committed members will strongly resist the demands imposed by
charismatic refounders. The "non-rational elements of the trans-
forming experience"[63] were *not* what they had bought into when
they entered, at the previous time of stable commitment mechanisms. They may perceive the refounding individual as initiating a
cult of personality, or as fostering psychological infantilism in
his/her followers. "After the disclaimers of guilt by obedient
Nazis at the Nuremberg trials," states Marie Augusta Neal, "reli-

gious men and women can no longer honestly idealize a total submission to the will of another human being as a good."[64] It is not at all inconceivable that members of a religious congregation would choose their organizational demise—in contradiction to the usual clinging to life which most organizations exhibit— rather than submit to a charismatic refounder. Or they may delude themselves that their order's revitalization is possible without the "excessive" demands which a charismatic refounding would impose. However, few if any of the intentional communities sociologists have studied have been able to survive and renew themselves without the kind of ideological commitment which charismatic refounders reawaken.

CONCLUSIONS

To the extent that twentieth century religious congregations continue to be intentional communities, they will be subject to the cyclic pattern of growth and decline that all religious congregations have followed throughout history. Most are currently in a decline phase, with many members experiencing alienation at the most profound level, and are questioning the relevance of their basic charisms. This situation is extremely threatening, however, and both the membership and the leaders may prefer to deny that it exists:

> The sense of corporate belonging is weak. Though religious may still live together, they work at different apostolates. Members are weary of having community meetings to discuss their future or how to improve community life; they just want to be left alone to survive. . . . It is better to live in peaceful co-existence and avoid recognizing our deep theological divisions.
>
> So community life is shallow and apt to be more to the "boarding house" or "gentlemen's club" style—pleasant, but definitely not threatening, for real issues that might divide are avoided and individual independence is carefully observed.[65]

For most congregations, the alienation and increased detachment of the current members has been exacerbated by a high rate of attrition and few new entrants. According to Neal, membership in women's religious congregations has declined thirty-three percent—from 181,421 in 1966 to 120,699 in 1983. Men's orders have declined fourteen percent, with the greatest loss among brothers (thirty-eight percent) rather than among priests (one percent).[66] This decline is more precipitous than at any time since the French Revolution (the decline phase of the last cycle).[67] Specific ministries have lost religious at an even greater rate: although there are thirty-three percent fewer women religious now than in 1966, there are sixty-eight percent fewer teaching in Catholic schools.[68]

Is refounding possible for these communities? Previous studies would seem to indicate that refounding is more likely for congregations oriented around a particular spirituality than for those oriented around a given work, since the former translates more readily into new contexts. Any refounding that does take place, however, will do so in an atmosphere of opposition, hostility and even schism. Great faith would be needed to continue to support refounding in these circumstances.

It is more likely, therefore, that new religious congregations, in new formats, will arise from the ashes of the former era. Many of the new forms may not be recognized as "real religious life" at first. Some, like the volunteers who staff the Covenant Houses for runaway youth in New York and other cities, may have rotating populations of temporary members. Others, like the charismatic community in Ann Arbor, Michigan, may appear cult-like to outsiders. And, in fact, many of these new forms may prove nonviable and disappear without making a major impact upon any newly-developing model of religious life. Those that succeed will be characterized by a relatively high growth rate, which eventually will lead to the same routinizing pressures that pushed previous forms of congregations toward the more traditional model. In time, the very characteristics that made them distinctive will shift back to some degree of conformity with traditional patterns, although a residue or flavor of their uniqueness will always remain.

Others of the newly founded congregations will claim to be returning to the pure spirit of traditional religious life, and will appear excessively conservative to members of more liberal communities. According to Hostie, the innovations these groups make in reinterpreting the traditional format of religious life may not be apparent even to the members themselves.[69] But some innovation, however unrecognized, is necessary. It is unlikely that a community that fails to innovate when returning to a purely traditional model will be able to meet the needs of a society which has radically diverged from the situation which had given birth to that model.

The trends hypothesized in the preceding paragraphs are applicable to religious congregations only to the extent that they continue to be intentional communities. This is an important qualification. Most religious congregations no longer completely conform to the communitarian model; they also contain many bureaucratic and associational elements. Indeed, the psychological liabilities of intentional communities may lead readers of this chapter to conclude, "If that's what an intentional community is like, heaven preserve us from refounding our community along that model. And pity the poor deluded souls who join the new ones!" Intentional communities do have serious liabilities as well as profound advantages as an organizational form for religious congregations. The next two chapters will consider two alternate forms of group organization, the association and the bureaucracy, to explore their potential as alternatives for religious life.

3

Bureaucratic Organization
and Religious Life

The Sociological Concept of Bureaucracy

In common usage, the term "bureaucratic" is unflattering. The bad reputation of bureaucracies dates back to the early nineteenth century, when liberal writers used the label "to decry the tortuous procedures, narrow outlook and highhanded manner of autocratic [government] officials."[1] Since then, the encyclopedia entry tells us, "bureaucratic" has been employed by critics of both left and right to describe any instance of "rigid rules and routines that are applied with little consideration of the specific case, of blundering officials, of slow operation and buck-passing, of conflicting directives and duplication of effort, of empire building and of concentration of control within the hands of a few."[2] Modern writers on religious life often make similar assumptions about bureaucracies. An article in a recent issue of *Human Development*, for example, describes "early bureaucratization" as being characterized by "backbiting, coalition building and paranoia . . . the structures and the planning and development functions are much less responsive. . . . Decentralization and delegation become increasingly threatening to leadership."[3] In the "late bureaucratization" stage, "miscommunication is commonplace, two-way communication is alien. . . . Administrative leadership struggles to buy time, to prolong the organization's life before its demise is imminent. Inefficiency and ineffectiveness are to be expected. Clients find that access to responsive subsystems is rare."[4] Bureaucratization, in the popular view, is a pathological state, and its unwelcome appearance is the herald of an organization's decay and ultimate extinction.

Sociological literature on bureaucracies takes a somewhat different view. According to Max Weber, who did much of the early writing on the subject, bureaucracy is a particularly effective type of organizational form which reached its present configuration in eighteenth and nineteenth century Europe and has since spread throughout the modern industrial world. The ascendancy of bureaucratic organization may or may not be desirable—Weber himself had misgivings on the subject—but its superior effectiveness has made it predominant. Most large organizations—in government, in business, and even in the charitable and ecclesiastical spheres—now conform to the Weberian model of bureaucracy to a greater or lesser extent. Religious congregations have also experienced the pressure to adopt bureaucratic characteristics, whether or not they "mix well" with the communitarian aspects of religious life.

CHARACTERISTICS OF BUREAUCRACIES

Division of Labor and a Hierarchy of Authority

In a bureaucratically-organized group, each member has a specific role, with one or more assigned tasks. A specialized job description is often available. The member's contributions are evaluated on the basis of this job description, and not on extraneous criteria such as the physical attractiveness of his/her spouse, or adherence to a particular political party. This feature of bureaucracies can be contrasted to the situation in pre-bureaucratic or non-bureaucratic groups: in Louis XVI's court, for example, the courtiers were "in waiting" upon the king, and could be commanded to perform a wide variety of functions—from drawing the royal bath one day to overseeing the royal treasury the next.[5] It is a peculiarity of modern western culture that we now look down upon employees who perform these generalized "servant" functions; the objections of corporate secretaries when asked to make their boss' coffee or pick out presents for his wife are attempts to transform the secretarial role from a pre-bureaucratic to a higher-status bureaucratic one.[6]

The meticulously-codified positions in a bureaucratized organization are arranged in a hierarchy of authority, with occupants of the upper positions having certain specific powers over those directly beneath them. This again differs from non-bureaucratic authority: your boss can demand that you arrive on time and adhere to certain standards of work (both of which demands would have been considered intolerable infringements on one's personal freedom as recently as the mid-nineteenth century),[7] but she cannot require that you watch certain television programs or marry a certain type of spouse. Also, the supervisor of one department has no authority over the subordinates in another: the head of Marketing cannot give orders to the secretaries in Personnel, and both the secretaries and the Director of Personnel would be infuriated if he tried to do so. Finally, the work authority of the superior over the subordinate in a modern bureaucracy rests on his/her position in the hierarchy, and not on possession of a charismatic personality (which the leader of an intentional community has to have) or on parentage or kin ties (as in a medieval court). Once a supervisor receives the requisite gold watch and retires, he relinquishes all ability to demand anything from his former subordinates.

Written Rules and Files

A bureaucratic organization lives on paper. The job descriptions, evaluation forms, and hierarchical flow charts described above imply an established written record, so that everyone knows exactly what is expected. An entire administrative level has been created to process these records: the ranks marked "clerical" and "administrative" in the U.S. census have swollen from about eight percent of the labor force in 1870 (when the United States was relatively unbureaucratized) to twenty-eight percent today.[8] Whatever Ebenezer Scrooge's business was, he had only one secretary to help him run it, and Andrew Carnegie did all of his own hiring and firing. Today Scrooge would have several office managers and an entire army of secretaries, and USX Corporation (the modern descendent of Carnegie's U.S. Steel) probably employs more persons in its various Personnel Departments alone than had worked in all of Carnegie's original factory. In the process of expanding its administrative level, management becomes further and further separated from the workers who produce the actual product of the organization, whether that product be cured hospital patients, eighth graders, or new cars.

Separation of Office and Incumbent

The occupant of a particular niche in a bureaucratically-structured organization is reimbursed by an established salary and does not usually profit from the job in other ways. As an example of this, one could compare the bureaucratized tax collection of the IRS with medieval tax collectors. The IRS employee is paid a fixed salary; any attempt to pocket the actual tax monies he or she collects would result in immediate dismissal and probably criminal prosecution. Tax collectors in the middle ages, by contrast, held franchises from their feudal lord, covering particular territories: they would then hire their own private guards to extort as much as they could from the populace. After sending the king or lord a fixed amount, they were permitted to keep the remainder.[9] No wonder tax collectors were so hated!

Universality of Treatment

The modern bureaucracy also operates impartially toward both its clients and its employees, at least in theory. All clients/ customers expect to be treated according to the same standard: the amount of money each one pays for a tube of toothpaste or the length of time each one waits for a public housing apartment should be equal. If the standard does vary, that variation should be codified according to pre-established rules, and not depend merely on the whims or personal preferences of sales clerks or public housing officials. Parenthetically, the codification of these rules adds another layer of paper files for the administrative level to manage. Employees, too, expect to be treated equally: they assume that the salary schedule will be applied uniformly within a particular level or rank, and that they will not be fired without cause.

Finally, and again in theory if not in practice, a bureaucracy avoids favoritism in its hiring and promotion procedures. The personnel department scrutinizes the qualifications of the applicants and hires the one best suited for the job, regardless of his or her extraneous characteristics. Once hired, the new employee's work is periodically rated (and written records are kept of these ratings) so that, when the next higher position in the hierarchy becomes vacant, the most capable occupant of the lower rungs can be promoted to fill it. In this way, the member of a bureaucratically-organized group can build up an entire career within its ranks, moving progressively to positions of ever-greater responsibility and remuneration.

ORGANIZATIONAL ADAPTATIONS AND DEVIATIONS

No organization ever conforms totally to the abstract theoretical model of a bureaucracy. Despite the confusion sometimes caused by his use of the term "ideal type" to describe this model, Weber never meant that real-life organizations ought to follow it exactly. His interest lay, rather, in seeing how organizations deviated from the theoretical model, and in uncovering what the reasons for these deviations might be. A particular non-bureaucratic practice may seem, on the surface, to be irrational, but it may actually prove to be more efficient. Or the staff may lack knowledge of how to achieve the bureaucratic ideal, and thus resort to non-bureaucratic shortcuts which yield a satisfactory, if not an optimum, outcome.[10] Or an unbureaucratic practice may enhance the power of a particular individual or group within the organization, and be adhered to for that reason. The arbitrary application of bureaucratic rules, for example, increases the power of a supervisor: the workers must stay on their supervisor's good side in order to avoid a crackdown.

In sociological writing, therefore, a bureaucracy is simply a more efficient way of organizing a group to perform its tasks. Other methods of organization have been devised in the past, and still others may arise in the future. The supposed negative characteristics of a bureaucracy do not arise from the bureaucratic form, *but rather out of the deviations from that form which emerge over time.* And these deviations, far from weakening the organization, may actually cause it to become stronger and better able to ensure its own survival in a changing or even a hostile environment. For this reason, the bureaucratic form has spread, both geographically and functionally, and occurs in societies ranging from the United States and France to Russia, Mexico and India, and in societal sectors such as hospitals, universities and religious denominations, as well as in its original strongholds of government and business. It remains to be seen, however, whether the widespread adoption of the bureaucratic form is suitable to the particular needs of the organizations involved.

Bureaucratic Organization and Religious Life

BUREAUCRATIZATION IN RELIGIOUS COMMUNITIES

In many ways, the bureaucratic model is the least congruent with traditional religious commitment, even though a number of bureaucratic elements have existed in the Catholic Church perhaps longer than anywhere else.[11] By its very nature, bureaucracy assumes the compartmentalization and segmentation of an individual's life. The worker in a bureaucratic organization is expected to perform only those activities within his or her job description, which implies that other responsibilities may be ignored as "someone else's job." The authority of the supervisors within the group is limited to the particular task at hand and does not extend to any influence over the beliefs and values of the subordinates, nor to their activities outside the deliberately limited purview of the organization. Individuals within a bureaucracy are expected to perform their jobs "sine ira et studio"—i.e. dispassionately and without allowing them to be colored by their own personal feelings. Finally, bureaucratic organization is most suitable for those tasks that can be precisely measured and evaluated.

In religious communities, by contrast, the individual is expected to commit his or her whole life, without reservation, to following in the footsteps of Christ—not merely the time period between 9 A.M. and 5 P.M., or the specific activities involved in teaching fifth graders or administering a hospital. Furthermore, the roles most central to religious life are precisely the ones which are least able to be measured. Previous attempts to do so, even in the communities' less bureaucratic days, resulted in some very serious distortions—preferring punctuality at prayers or the strict observance of silence to true charity, for example. When a bureaucracy is faced with having to measure an unmeasurable trait, it tends to substitute a more measurable one. Several sociological studies have traced this process in a wide variety of organizational settings—such as the substitution of "number of forms completed" for "helping clients" when evaluating the effectiveness of a state social welfare agency.[12] Similarly, dioceses have often substituted "seminarians' academic grades" for their "holiness" or their (as yet unascertained) "administrative ability" when determining who will be sent to Rome for study and for placement on the fast track from which bishops are later drawn.[13] There is little evidence that the substituted measurable criteria coincide with the unmeasurable ones, or that, therefore, bureaucratic procedures are the best way to operate in these instances.

Despite this incompatibility, some bureaucratization has always existed in religious communities, embedded as they are in the bureaucratized structure of the larger church. The number of bureaucratic elements began to increase, however, in the decades before Vatican II, and has progressed to such an extent that a wide variety of bureaucratic procedures are taken for granted today, both in running an order's ministries and in the operation of the congregation itself. Beginning at least with the Sister Formation Movement of the 1950s, the desirability of having individual members professionally prepared for their ministerial positions was recognized by congregations of women religious in this country.[14] This meant that a sister's credentials and experience, and not merely the desire of her superior or the needs of the community, helped to determine her appointment to a particular position—an example of the application of bureaucratic standards of hiring and promotion. The high value placed on bureaucratically impartial hiring standards has become, if anything, more widespread since the 1950s. The possession of accepted professional credentials, rather than non-bureaucratic criteria such as membership in the congregation itself, is now the most important prerequisite for many ministerial positions, jobs which had formerly been the exclusive preserve of the religious of the sponsoring order. The top positions in many congregationally-owned universities and hospitals are now occupied by lay men and women on the basis of their stronger professional qualifications. Not only is this not questioned, it is seen as desirable and just. Ministerial institutions have also increased their written records (having a written personnel handbook, or using standard double-entry bookkeeping, for example). And the religious employees of a school or hospital often live elsewhere and enjoy the same 9 to 5 work day as their lay colleagues, in contrast to former days when they lived "above the store." The ministerial institutions—the schools, hospitals, chancery offices, and the like—in which religious work may thus be indistinguishable from their secular counterparts, at least insofar as their organizational form is concerned. Both the lay and the religious employees probably prefer it that way, and would resist any attempt to reinstate pre-bureaucratic procedures.

Additional bureaucratization has also occurred within religious communities. Many Superiors General (now often called "Presidents"—the change of term is significant) and their councillors no longer live at the Motherhouse where they work. Formal job descriptions are written for their positions. An administrative sector begins to grow, parallel to the expansion of white collar and clerical work in business. According to Marie Augusta Neal's figures, most congregations have a larger percentage of their active membership in congregational administration now (3.5%) than they had twenty years ago (2.2%), even though the overall number of members to be served is smaller.[15] Bureaucratization within religious congregations has been less extensive than the bureaucratization of their ministries. But it has continued to grow.

REASONS FOR BUREAUCRATIZATION IN RELIGIOUS COMMUNITIES

The "Myth of Bureaucracy"

Why have religious communities adopted additional bureaucratic forms of organization, especially since such forms are often alien to their original ideology and beliefs? One possible reason may be because the transcendent good of bureaucratic forms has become a basic value of western culture, and one which most religious also accept.[16] An organization, even a religious one, may *have* to adopt bureaucratic methods in order to be taken seriously by the surrounding culture. If a business did not have a separate accounting or personnel department, if a hospital had no segmentation between the roles of nurses, doctors and janitors, if a school hired as teachers whoever the principal thought would work well with children, they would be severely penalized. Banks might not extend them credit, customers or clients might refuse to use their services, and their employees might go on strike over their unfair labor practices. In some cases, bureaucratic procedures are legislated by the government: a school or hospital is required to hire only specifically qualified persons to practice medicine or teach the children, and the IRS would look askance on any business that did not employ accepted accounting techniques. In other words, even though *bureaucracy* has a bad reputation in American culture, many bureaucratic *practices* do not. Instead, such practices are labeled "scientific" or "fair" and prescribed in a wide variety of situations.

It must be remembered, however, that the putative superiority of bureaucratic procedures may be a myth. The emergency room nurse may know more than the resident doctor—her bureaucratic superior. Artificially separating the research and development department from a company's sales department may put the former out of touch with what customers really want, and may inhibit beneficial cross-fertilization of ideas. Similarly, in religious communities, writing segmented job descriptions for the president and council might lead to the neglect of the less readily codifiable aspects of their roles. Or it might inhibit cooperation and information sharing. But the prevalence of job descriptions in the surrounding culture may encourage their creation in religious congregations as well.

Once bureaucratic procedures are adopted in an organization, even if they are basically dysfunctional, they will tend to perpetuate themselves. A newly-created department will develop a specialized vocabulary and an ever-increasing number of professional tasks in order to legitimize its existence.[17] As more and more of the institutions in the environment adopt a particular practice or establish a particular department, "isomorphism," or fitting in with what everyone else does, will be necessary in order to stabilize one's own organization. If, for example, business schools train their students to work in organizations that are structured in a certain way, it will be difficult for a differently-arranged institution to find qualified employees. Or professional associations may assume standard configurations of skills and interests, which would make them less beneficial to members whose backgrounds cross disciplinary boundaries.

A final reason for the adoption and retention of bureaucratic procedures may be in order to make some response to unpredictable and changing environmental conditions. At such times, an organization, not knowing how to react, may cling to "scientifically-proven," superior, bureaucratic procedures as an assurance that at least they are doing something—the *best* thing, the *proven* thing—to deal with the crisis. In religious congregations faced by declining numbers of new members, for example, the first reaction may be to set up a separate vocation office, complete with a full-time director, job description, etc. While there is evidence that this bureaucratization helps somewhat,[18] it certainly has not solved the problem. The communitarian or the associational model may provide more effective methods for addressing recruitment of new members, methods which the bureaucratic model will not consider.

According to the above hypothesis, therefore, bureaucratic procedures may persist in many organizations because of outside pressures, even if they are fundamentally incongruent with the basic needs or values of the group. The bureaucratization of the ministries and the internal processes of a religious community may indeed be beneficial. But its desirability should be carefully examined and evaluated.

Bureaucracy as a Powerful Tool

The assertion that bureaucracy is a mere ceremonial accretion to the real work of an organization—adopted only because of outside pressure—is not universally accepted. Other writers argue that its nearly universal use is the result of the concrete benefits it offers. For Max Weber, modern western bureaucracy is the social equivalent of the invention of the wheel, as far superior to other ways of getting things done "as machine manufacture is to non-mechanical modes of production."[19] Bureaucracy is never uninvented in an organization; once adopted, it is *never* discarded. The bureaucratically-based division of labor helps eliminate wasteful duplication of services; job descriptions and universalistic hiring help attract and promote the most qualified people. Written files become an indispensable way of keeping track of what is going on. It would be simply impossible, Weber said, to sustain the productivity of modern western society without bureaucratization. Thus, this school of thought would assert that, as religious orders entered upon their greatest period of membership expansion in the 1950s and early 1960s, it was "almost inevitable" that further bureaucratization occurred, both to keep up with all that needed to be done in the ministry, and to organize the ever-larger number of members.[20]

In addition to its usefulness in structuring the work and the operations of an organization more efficiently, bureaucratic procedures are also very effective at enhancing power—both of the organization as a whole and of particular individuals within it. This power advantage has implications, first of all, for the relationship between a bureaucratized organization and its external environment. Through the large-scale operations made possible by bureaucratization, a business can influence a community's tax system and road placement, or even to keep other businesses out and destroy neighborhoods, thus altering its surrounding environment to its own advantage.[21] In the struggle, groups which are not bureaucratically organized tend to be smaller and weaker, and may ultimately be forced to die or disband. The bureaucratic reliance on universal standards and professional credentials can also be a source of power. Periodically throughout their existence, religious congregations have faced opposition, both from bishops and priests as well as from non-church groups. Appeal to bureaucratic standards may have helped them to protect their own interests:

> The struggle to upgrade sisters' education to better prepare them for the classroom, and, as time went by, to meet state certification standards, replaced canonical status and autonomy as the single greatest source of tension between bishops and communities in the first half of the twentieth century.[22]

An Evaluation of the Bureaucratic Model for Religious Congregations

Whether because of bureaucratizing pressures from the surrounding environments or because of the superior efficiency and power advantages of the bureaucratic model, religious congregations have adopted it extensively in their ministerial organizations as well as in their own internal operations. There are both positive and negative aspects to this. The next section of this chapter will point out ways in which the bureaucratic model differs from the intentional community model, and then explore the strengths and weaknesses of each.

DIFFERENCES BETWEEN BUREAUCRATIC AND COMMUNITARIAN MODELS

Segmentation of Roles

A primary difference between the bureaucratic and the intentional community models is the segmentalized and codified commitment structure of the former, as compared to the all-encompassing demands made by the latter. There is a clearly-defined limit to what a bureaucracy can demand of its members, especially in areas not directly related to the instrumental tasks for which the group was originally created. Even within the formal work sphere, the power of a bureaucratic hierarchy over its subordinates may be limited. Lower-level workers are often quite skilled at using seniority regulations or safety standards to carve out for themselves areas of autonomy on the job. The rationalized and limited commitment structure of bureaucracies has been accepted by American culture as good, and attempts to enforce the all-encompassing demands of an intentional community would be intensely resisted in most bureaucratically-organized groups.

But religious congregations still retain the basic ideology and value system of their communitarian origins; the fundamental rationale for entering religious life—"Sell all you have and follow me"—implies the *total* commitment which only an intentional community may demand. As has been pointed out in the previous chapter, however, intentional communities can be psychologically dangerous for their members, precisely because the autonomy of the individual is so subordinated to the needs of the group. Most religious can cite examples of the abuse of individual rights within their congregation. The potential for this abuse still exists, as long as the order remains an intentional community in form. Bureaucracies, by definition, were created to limit and define the authority of the group over the individual. For this reason, early in the history of religious communities, formal provisions were written into canon law to harness religious charisma within the bureaucratic structures of the larger church.[23] More recently, many congregations have adopted further bureaucratic traits such as grievance procedures, personnel departments, and administrative job descriptions precisely in order to defuse the explosive potential of the totalistic demands of an intentional community.

The problem then arises of which standard to apply—the bureaucratic or the communitarian one—in the exercise of the congregation's leadership. General and regional superiors (or presidents and personnel directors) may have little difficulty establishing and enforcing financial policies, retirement regulations and the like, since these responsibilities are delegated to the leadership under both models. But spiritual or value-directed roles will be harder to exercise, since they are incongruent with the bureaucratic model while being simultaneously required by the communitarian one. In such a situation, leadership may engage in "decoupling," that is, isolating from exposure to detailed scrutiny or evaluation those intentional community aspects of their roles for which there is no bureaucratic foundation.[24] One example of decoupling is to couch goals or standards in such ambiguous language that a wide variety of actions can appear to conform to them. The vow of obedience, for example, becomes defined as openness to the guidance of the Holy Spirit in one's life (which can be reasonably claimed by any member), rather than as submission to the wishes of particular individuals in specifically-defined situations (which the leadership would then have to enforce, against the probable resistance of those members who no longer ascribe to the congregation that degree of control over their lives). Another decoupling technique is to ceremonialize inspection and evaluation. Regional superiors may make yearly visits, and monthly house meetings may be held, but the topics for discussion are carefully chosen. Participants avoid anything which would reveal the basic discrepancy between the hypothetical communal authority which the group may have over the members' non-work lives, and the *actual* authority which the members are willing to cede to it under the present, more bureaucratized structure.

Religious congregations, precariously balanced between the competing commitment models of bureaucracies and intentional communities, may thus have mutually contradictory expectations of their leadership or of their members. This may have deleterious effects. For example, certain aspects of the leadership role (especially the prophetic function of challenging the members to a deeper living out of their religious commitment) may be ignored, because no one wants to return to the way in which these aspects used to be addressed under the intentional community model. Congregations which refrain from addressing the ambiguous roles of the leadership may miss discovering creative and psychologically healthy new ways of filling them. Ordinary members, on the other hand, may give less weight to the pronouncements of their leaders for which there is little bureaucratic justification. As long as religious congregations combine elements of both bureaucracies and intentional communities, a certain amount of tension will exist in the contradictory expectations which each of these models places on both the leadership and the average members.

Efficiency vs. the Primacy of Other Values

A second difference between the communitarian and the bureaucratic models is the stress which the latter places on efficiency. For Weber, in fact, this was a key identifying characteristic of the bureaucratic form: the primary standard by which all of the other characteristics of a bureaucracy are measured is their superior effectiveness at attaining the goal(s) of the organization, when compared to other means of doing so.[25] It is simply more efficient, he stated, to have specialized job descriptions so that efforts are not duplicated, to hire the most capable people, and to keep track of policies in written files rather than to rely on potentially fallible and conflicting memories of what the policies were. Less bureaucratized groups are more likely to include other values besides efficiency in their workings—to hire kin on the basis of family loyalty, perhaps, or to enforce unwritten rules in order to increase group solidarity. These non-bureaucratic practices may lead to less efficient modes of operation, and may penalize those organizations which cling to them.

But no intentional community was ever founded to be efficient. Especially in their beginnings, efficiency is subordinated to "higher" values: in Israeli kibbutzim, for example, all jobs were originally rotated so that no one member could monopolize the high prestige positions. For the early kibbutz members, therefore, the transcendent value was equality, and this took precedence over mere efficiency. In other intentional communities, the key value may be the achievement of spiritual perfection or the maintenance of loving relationships among the members. But in the long run, efficiency tends to win out over these other values. Recent research on kibbutzim has documented a gradual drift toward a very stable—and unequal—division of labor: the women members now largely work in less prestigious occupations such as kitchen work and child care, while, among the men, the holders of certain jobs have greater access to cars, travel opportunities and the like.[26] Jobs are rotated less frequently, if at all, since their current occupants have built up a certain amount of expertise in them. There is a limit to how long an intentional community can ignore the demands of efficiency before problems of coordination and daily functioning develop. This is especially true for the teaching congregations of the most recent age of religious life, since a primary reason for their founding was to render a particular service in the church. Every religious above a certain age can probably cite horror stories of persons who were simply placed in a ministry whether or not they were capable of doing the work: the "grace of office" did not always enable these individuals to operate effectively in their new positions, and often had tragic personal and ministerial consequences. Over time, therefore, all intentional communities have to make some compromises between efficiency and their other values, in order to obtain, in a competitive environment, enough resources for survival.

Again, the position in which many religious congregations find themselves—of straddling the fence between the bureaucratic and the communitarian commitment models—leads to some difficult questions. By what criteria, for example, does one determine the "best" person for a congregational position—the most prophetic? the most compassionate? the most organized? the most professionally qualified? (And how would one measure compassion, anyway, to determine who had the "most" of it? But in speaking of *measuring*, we are getting bureaucratic again . . .) What other values are more important than efficiency—love? familial togetherness? prayer? And at what point must these other values be sacrificed so that essential tasks get done? On the one hand, strict adherence to bureaucratic standards of universality and efficiency will seem very cold and impersonal to members who have communitarian leanings, while, on the other hand, disregard of efficiency in personnel considerations or in operating procedures is likely to drive other members to distraction.

Flexibility

Intentional communities do tend to be inflexible, especially once their original founders have passed from the scene and the traditional commitment mechanisms increase in importance. *But bureaucracies are often just as inflexible.* This inflexibility stems from certain real-world limitations on the theoretical ability of a bureaucratic organization to choose the best course of action, and to change it should environmental conditions ever change. In order thoroughly to conform to the ideal model, decision makers in a bureaucracy would need to know what mix of skills would be the best to look for in a potential employee, or what type of product would be most in demand among its customers. But often this information is simply not available. And the "search costs" of trying to discover the optimum solutions would be prohibitive, even if such solutions could be found at all. So decision makers search only long enough to find a "satisfactory" solution, among a limited number of the alternatives most immediately available to them.

> The organizational and social environment in which the decision maker finds himself determines what consequences he will anticipate, what ones he will not; what alternatives he will consider, what ones he will ignore.[27]

The decision thus reached may not be the best one, but it will become enshrined in the "programs" which the organization will use thereafter when confronted by a similar situation. A university admissions department will thus send its staff to the same set of high schools year after year, because that is where its students came from in the past. A hospital will habitually order its supplies from the same supplier; a business will tend to promote into upper management employees from the sales department rather than persons from other departments. Over time, therefore, the behavior of an organization becomes very predictable:

> Knowledge of the program of an organization permits one to predict in considerable detail the behavior of members of the organization. And the greater the programming of individual activities in the organization, the greater the predictability of these activities.[28]

This programming limits the ability of an organization to respond to change. The mindset of the program may, first of all, prevent the decision makers from even noticing that a change has occurred; there always exists a certain tendency to interpret slightly discrepant phenomena in terms of what is already familiar. Even if the new situation is recognized for what it is, decision makers may be inhibited by their programs from being sufficiently creative to find a solution. And, within the organization, whole departments will have grown up that have a vested interest in the programmed status quo. Strong political pressures will militate against too novel or too disruptive a solution.

Both bureaucracies and intentional communities, therefore, are inflexible, if perhaps in different ways and for different reasons. It is important to remember this, because the limits on bureaucratic members' decision making, while no less real than those on intentional community members, are often less easy to perceive. The subordination of the individual to the larger group is an established part of the communitarian ideology. In a bureaucracy, on the other hand, members may sincerely believe that they have a great deal of personal autonomy, or that they have thoroughly considered all possible alternatives before making a decision. It is safe for the organization to allow this autonomy, however, because the organization's programs constrict the members' vision in such a way that it occurs to them to consider only certain alternatives. The most effective control is unobtrusive control.[29]

For religious congregations, it will be important to remember the limitations on flexibility inherent in both of these models. In the past twenty years, religious communities have faced fundamental environmental changes—changes that may threaten their very survival. Creative solutions are urgently needed, but neither the bureaucratic nor the communitarian model is likely to provide them. With regard to declining entrance rates, for example, a community's members may be unable even to conceive of a different way of addressing the problem, other than the bureaucratic one of setting up a department to attend to it. Their established programs may blind them to alternatives as completely as the commitment mechanisms blind intentional communities.

ORGANIZATIONAL OUTCOMES

In the final section of this chapter, I would like to consider some of the concrete outcomes, positive and negative, which the addition of bureaucratic elements has created for religious life. Each congregation, of course, will have a slightly different mix of these elements, and thus the potential outcomes will vary somewhat in each case. The overall view presented here should be modified as it applies to a particular situation.

The Effects of Bureaucratization on Power

Bureaucracies are both sources of power and arenas in which power is wielded. The modern bureaucratic model is especially designed to limit the unbalanced accumulation of power in any organizational sector, including the top levels. Far from overly restricting subordinates, for example, the written rules and job descriptions of a bureaucracy can actually enable them to exercise responsibility within a defined sphere, freed from arbitrary employer interference.[30] In non-bureaucratized settings, by contrast, employers have more power and employees have less. Rosabeth Moss Kanter, for example, has documented the arbitrary and diffuse patrimonial authority which corporate executives have over their personal secretaries, a power which would have been severely reduced had formal bureaucratic job descriptions been drawn up for these women.[31] A study of Southern Baptist ministers found a similar situation: these men strongly resisted the formal delineation of their roles and those of their staffs, since this would have limited their power.[32] The bureaucratic division of labor can also lead to an employee's specialization in key organizational tasks. If this specialization renders the employee irreplaceable, his/her power vis-à-vis the larger organization would be enhanced. Finally, the clearly-defined career paths implied by the bureaucratic hierarchy and impartial promotion standards allow at least some workers to advance over time to positions of greater authority and responsibility. Nominal subordinates who are on a "fast track" of career advancement can garner power and influence out of proportion to their current position, as fellow workers jockey for alliances with them.

Such findings have implications for the empowerment of members of religious congregations, especially congregations of women. Most women religious have been accustomed to working in ministries run by their own orders, where the bureaucratization of the 1950s and 1960s had resulted in written job descriptions and recognized areas of professional competence. Such procedures enhanced the power of the sisters working in the lower ranks by limiting the authority of their supervisors (religious or lay) to certain specified areas only. If these sisters accept an essentially undefined "go-fer" job as a pastoral associate, they are quite likely to become disillusioned, as their relative powerlessness and their non-bureaucratic dependence on the whim of the pastor become evident. There is a surprising lack of data on the extent of this dissatisfaction. Currently, there are no statistics on the drop-out rate of pastoral associates, nor on the average length of time they spend in one parish. Perhaps this lack of information stems from the fact that religious congregations are not used to thinking of themselves as bureaucratic organizations, and are unaware of the implications for empowerment which are inherent in the bureaucratic model. The data on turnover rates among pastoral associates may be present in the personnel files, but no one may have thought to retrieve and analyze it, or to warn potential parish workers ahead of time of the potential for disempowerment inherent in some of these positions. Worse still, the data may never have been recorded in the first place.

The Effects of Bureaucratization on Counter-Cultural Witness

For several reasons, a largely bureaucratized religious congregation is less likely than an intentional community to witness to (or even to maintain within itself) the counter-cultural aspects of its ideology. Theoretically, at least, a bureaucratic organization does not attempt to control its members' private lives, which includes not interfering in whatever personal beliefs and values they may have. As long as an employee does his or her work, it does not matter whether he or she believes in ghosts, marries a person of another race, or likes to read pornographic magazines. In hybridized bureaucratic-communitarian religious life, *it is only through its communitarian elements* that a congregation retains any right to expect uniformity of its members concerning their interpretation of the vision of the founder, the desirability of poverty (or of celibacy, or of common prayer), or any of its other formerly key values. As the communitarian elements of a congregation diminish in importance (which they tend to do in practice some time before the official documents of the order reflect their disappearance), common values and beliefs will also diminish. This is especially likely when religious, working as they do in less isolated work settings than the congregationally-staffed institutions of thirty years ago, are exposed to the beliefs and values of their lay colleagues. As commonality of beliefs and values among the members becomes more tenuous, "decoupling" will occur, and the ideology of the community will be reinterpreted in more general language which can be more readily assimilated into the mainstream culture. Whether or not counter-cultural witness is preferable to inculturation is an open question, but bureaucratically-organized congregations will find themselves more likely to be doing the latter than the former.

Bureaucratization is also a mainstream value in itself, and, by adopting it over other forms of organization, religious communities are discarding another dimension in which they could have been counter-cultural. Recently, there has been a certain amount of literature criticizing bureaucracy as a principle of organization.[33] These writers point out that the supposed efficiency of a bureaucratic organization may in fact be an ideology designed to serve the needs of those who currently hold its top positions. It was only in the twentieth century that working, not for oneself, or for a hereditary lord, or even for a capitalist robber baron, but rather for a fellow paid employee-manager became common. Since these managers did not themselves own the company, they needed an ideology to explain why the workers should listen to them. The reason they chose to emphasize was rationality and efficiency—their knowledge of the "one best way" to organize the workplace. Feminist authors, as well as other critics, find this belief paternalistic: "The evolving 'spirit of managerialism' was infused with a 'masculine ethic.' "[34]

> This "masculine ethic" elevates the traits assumed to belong to some men as necessities for effective management: a tough-minded approach to problems; analytic abilities to abstract and plan; a capacity to set aside personal, emotional considerations in the interests of task accomplishment; and a cognitive superiority in problem-solving and decision-making. These characteristics supposedly belonged to men, but then, practically all managers were men from the beginning. However, when women tried to enter management jobs, the masculine ethic was invoked as an exclusionary principle.[35]

Women in management became ghettoized in parts of the bureaucratized work force such as personnel departments, where their "feminine empathy" could best be used. By the same token, Personnel became a "dead end" position, for the characteristics it was thought to emphasize were antithetical to hard-nosed management.[36]

In contrast to the promotion standards prevalent in bureaucratized businesses, many religious, especially prior to 1960, were assigned to management-level positions in schools and hospitals on bases other than rational efficiency. For women religious, this gave them an opportunity for administrative experience rare among their secular counterparts. Even after the increased bureaucratization of religious ministries, the career track to management was often kept open for community members. As recently as 1984, almost all of the female CEOs listed in the directory of the American College of Hospital Administrators were nuns.[37] Some women religious were mentored into the top positions in hospitals and schools out of lower-level positions as nurses and teachers, positions from which there is normally little upward mobility.[38] Other nuns were simply assigned to management positions. I once interviewed a sister who was plucked from teaching business courses in her order's high school in 1968 and sent to administer a small hospital in upstate New York. She remained in that position for over six years, without formal training, and did very well. Several sociologists have contended that the need for a professional degree in order to fill bureaucratic administrative positions is largely a myth—that one can learn what is necessary just as easily on the job and that the required credentials are a way of screening out the non-elites rather than the non-qualified.[39] The mentoring system which operated in the less-bureaucratized ministerial institutions that religious orders used to run thus provided a structural avenue by which persons who would otherwise never have risen to key administrative posts because of their gender or their class background could have that opportunity. While this mobility ladder was initially retained when ministerial institutions bureaucratized, it has more recently become a casualty of the increased bureaucratization of many religious orders.

The more thorough bureaucratization of the ministerial institutions run by religious orders has therefore closed off alternative bases of organization and promotion, at precisely the time when other groups in society are attempting to recover them. In addition to the feminist critics already mentioned, for example, an entire army of analysts are attempting to duplicate in this country the Japanese methods of management by consensus.[40] Of course, it must be pointed out that religious congregations may not have had any choice but to adopt some of the main features of bureaucracies in their ministries: state laws increasingly mandate the possession of administrative credentials before one can take one's place at the top of health and education bureaucracies such as those run by religious orders. And for many organizational activities, bureaucracies really are more efficient. The challenge remains for religious orders to adopt sufficient bureaucratic procedures to profit from their benefits, without simultaneously experiencing their liabilities.

Conclusions

Religious congregations, then, are partly intentional communities and partly bureaucracies. As such, they sometimes face the difficulty of reconciling two contradictory standards when choosing a course of action. Each model has particular strengths and weaknesses. Bureaucracy's universalistic rules help check the potential for abuse of authority inherent in intentional communities. The bureaucratic division of labor, job descriptions and hiring on the basis of credentials help to eliminate duplication of effort and at least some of the likelihood that members will be saddled with jobs they are not able to handle. Intentional communities, on the other hand, are more capable of inspiring the level of dedication that seems congruent with the gospel message, something which the deliberately limited bureaucratic sphere does not appear capable of doing. And intentional communities are much more likely to support any counter-cultural witness which a community feels called to do; although this sort of witness is certainly possible in a bureaucracy, it is more difficult.

There is, however, yet a third group model to consider: the association, which is less rigorous in its demands on members than either of the two models discussed so far. Associations also have particular strengths and weaknesses. The next chapter will explore what they are, and what their implications may be for the evolution of religious life.

4

The Associational Model
and Religious Life

Definition and Discussion of Terms

In many ways, the associational model is the most applicable one
for religious congregations in the post-Vatican II era—more so,
even, than the intentional community. As one sociologist, herself
a former member of a religious community, recently wrote:

> ... religious orders emerged in the late 1960's and early
> 1970's as radically transformed institutions. While the three
> vows remained, they were interpreted to place less emphasis
> on self-denial and greater focus on the human and community
> dimensions of the vows. The hierarchical notion of superior
> and inferior was replaced by that of dialog among groups and
> individuals. The stress on cloister and isolation from the
> world gave way to emphasis on availability and witness in the
> world. ... *In short, the religious order changed from a total
> institution par excellence to a contemporary form of voluntary
> organization committed to providing resources to members.*[1]
> [italics mine]

What, exactly, is this associational model, along whose lines
many communities have reconstituted themselves? Elsewhere, I
have defined an association as "a group of persons who have
invested a certain amount of their resources in the attainment of

some common goal or objective, but who retain more personal autonomy and competing loyalties than would be possible in an intentional community."[2] In contrast to an intentional community, membership in an association allows for the possibility of other competing foci for one's attention and attachment: marital ties, for example, or work commitments, as well as ties to other associations. Members of associations are usually financially independent of them in a way that intentional community members are not: except for an administrative core (which is probably bureaucratic rather than associational in form), they receive no salaries or living stipends from their membership. Nor do they have any financial obligations to the association, beyond some fixed yearly dues. Associations, therefore, are non-totalistic in their demands on their members.

Associations are usually less able to be counter-cultural than intentional communities are, although there are some instances where this is not the case. Motorcycle gang members, for example, maintain a lifestyle that is largely at variance with mainstream American culture. So, for that matter, do very activist members of the nuclear disarmament movement, or some members of California "New Age" groups. Whenever the lifestyle of association members diverges radically from what is expected by the larger culture, however, it is likely that their association possesses some distinctive characteristics which most other associations do not. The association may be very similar to an intentional community, for example: the members of the motorcycle gang may all live in the same area (or even in the same building) and may spend almost all of their time together. Or the members may belong to several similar organizations with overlapping rosters: a set of peace activists may belong to Pax Christi *and* Greenpeace *and* SANE/ Freeze. The combined round of the meetings and activities of these organizations may absorb a large portion of the members' time, and their friends may all be drawn from these groups. Similarly, studies of some fundamentalist churches have found that, for very active members, their church affiliation provides them with a whole constellation of memberships, friends and activities.[3] The ability of an association to elicit counter-cultural behaviors and attitudes from its members thus depends on the extent to which that association—or an allied group of similar associations —is able to replicate the intentional community's insulation of its membership from competing value systems.

An association also differs from a bureaucracy. There are fewer formalized rules and job descriptions, and the hierarchy, if one exists at all, has less power to demand compliance from the members. Except for the bureaucratized central core, members work only voluntarily for the association, and receive no salary for what they do. Unlike bureaucracies, associations may be openly particularistic with regard to whom they admit to their ranks—the Daughters of the American Revolution excludes almost all non-WASPs, while several businessmen's clubs remain exclusively male. In real-life associations, many permutations can also occur which mix in bureaucratic and communitarian elements. A wide range of commitment levels may thus exist within the model, and even within a single association—wider than would be possible for the members of bureaucracies or intentional communities.

Associations, of course, differ among themselves along other dimensions. Their purposes may be expressive or instrumental, and, if instrumental, they may attempt to obtain benefits either for the members themselves, or else for the larger society (at least as the members define "benefit"). Alcoholics Anonymous and Weight Watchers would be examples of instrumental associations devoted to self-help; Amnesty International, the National Rifle Association, and Mothers Against Drunk Driving have societal goals. Many associations, of course, combine both instrumental and expressive goals. Associations also vary more widely in size than either bureaucracies or intentional communities do. And they vary in their location at the "center" or on the "periphery" of society, according to how much power and influence they possess.

Two Views of Associations

ASSOCIATIONS AS LESS DESIRABLE

If bureaucracies have a bad name in popular usage, associations also have been considered undesirable when compared to other group forms—not only by the public at large, but also by sociologists. Associations are the typical stronghold of secondary relationships, or "weak ties," which differ from the strong, intimate relationships prevalent in primary groups. By the "strength" of a relationship, sociologists mean the amount of time two individuals spend together, the emotional intensity of their interactions, their intimacy (mutual sharing) and the reciprocal services they can offer each other.[4] Strong ties are more likely in small primary groups like the family, a small village, or a college fraternity house. In both popular and sociological thought, strong, primary ties have been assumed to be better than weak ones. For example, television and motion pictures have romanticized life on Walton's Mountain, in Walnut Grove, or in Anatevka, "where I know everyone I meet." The Waltons and the Ingalls were thought to be more moral, more mentally healthy and closer as a family, because they were members of close-knit, primary groups.

In contrast, both sociologists and the public at large assumed that urban life was less desirable, precisely because the wholesome influences of primary groups would be lessened by the large size, increased density and social heterogeneity of the city.[5] Urbanites divided their time among a variety of associations—work, clubs, church, professional groups—without committing themselves entirely to any. The city dweller paid a high price for his/her increased individual freedom and detachment: alienation, anomie, moral decay, increased nervous tension and loneliness. Despairing young women could commit suicide in their apartments and no one would notice for days (a theme of several O. Henry stories; the coldness of the city complements the warmth of the country as a frequent topic in popular culture), while others could be murdered on the streets and no one would come to their aid. One sociologist even argued that the anonymity of urban life was what had predisposed the Germans to submit to the influence of Adolf Hitler.[6]

THE STRENGTH OF WEAK TIES

Recent writers, however, have questioned this assumption of the unremitting detrimental effects of secondary relationships.[7] These authors argue that "weak ties"—links to persons whom one knows in one particular context, but with whom one is not intimate—actually possess strengths and confer benefits that strong ties do not. Since weak ties are the kind most prevalent in associations, it would be good to study their characteristics, in order to apply them to increasingly associational religious congregations.

Patterns of Strong and Weak Ties

If two individuals (call them A and B) are linked by a strong tie, it is likely that they will also have a large proportion of their other friends in common. This is true because if A is a close friend of B and also a friend of C, the amount of time C can spend with A will be limited to the time A is not preoccupied with B, unless B, C, and A all spend time together. Also, the stronger the tie between A and B, and between A and C, the more similar A's two friends are likely to be to A, in tastes, interests and the like. This means that B and C are probably also similar to each other, and thus more likely to become friends once they meet. Finally, if B and A are close friends, and if B does not like C, this would upset B's "cognitive balance." B might become jealous of the time A and C spent together, and would be unable to understand what A saw in C, anyway. The closer B is to A, and the more alike they are in taste and temperament, the more confusing it would be for B to see A obviously enjoying the company of someone B did not like.[8] Thus, individuals whose relationship network is composed mainly of strong ties tend to be part of a primary group of close friends, all of whom interact more with each other than they do with outsiders.

While strong ties tend to clump individuals into isolated cliques of mutual friends, weak ties often form bridges between otherwise encapsulated groups. Figure 1 contrasts these two situations:

Figure 1

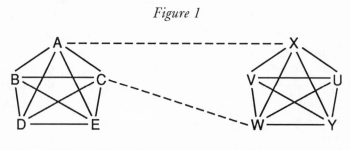

(Adapted from Granovetter, 1973, p. 1365.)

In the two friendship networks depicted here, (ABCDE and UVWXY), it is the "bridges"—the weak ties linking C with W and A with X—that open these otherwise isolated groups outside of themselves. Perhaps C and W work together, or maybe A and X go to the same church. While they do not know each other well, their nodding acquaintance may be a useful way of spreading information and even assistance between their respective groups.

Not all weak ties are bridges between primary groups—some connect social isolates, for example—but such bridges can be used to create paths between individuals in different networks, and to allow for the diffusion of information and ideas between groups. Granovetter hypothesizes that diffusion through weak ties travels farther and reaches more people than diffusion through strong ties.[9] In a more tightly-knit, encapsulated group, everyone would hear the same news two or three times, but it would go no farther.

Some creative research has been done on how American

society is linked through weak ties.[10] In these "Small World" experiments, an individual was given a booklet and told to send it to an arbitrarily chosen other individual. However, the booklet could not be sent directly, but only to someone whom the first person knew personally, and who might know the target individual. Thus, for example, a college student in California might be asked to get the booklet to President Bush, using only personal connections. The student might send it to her father, who would give it to his boss, who would send it to a business acquaintance in the D.C. area, who would hand it to a lobbyist, and so on. Of the completed chains, the links ranged between two and ten, with an average of five to eight.[11] The chains that went through weak ties were usually much more effective, and completed more quickly, than those that used strong ties.

Implications of Weak Ties for Individuals

In general, the more weak ties an individual has, the more ideas, influences and information he or she can get from socially distant sources.[12] Strong ties, on the other hand, are more reliable in times of real need (when one needs a thousand dollars in a hurry, for example, or when one has been evicted from one's apartment and needs a place to stay), but these situations are apt to be relatively infrequent in the lives of most middle class Americans. Poor people, therefore, are more likely to rely on strong ties, whereas business and professional persons will utilize more weak ones.[13]

> It follows that individuals with few weak ties will be deprived of information from different parts of the social system and will be confined to the provincial news and views of their close friends. This will not only insulate them from the latest ideas and fashions, but also put them in a disadvantaged position in the labor market, where advancement can depend . . . on knowing about appropriate job openings at just the right time.[14]

Weak ties, then, are an important resource for facilitating upward mobility in one's job.[15] Granovetter even speculates that destroying a weak tie will do more harm to a network than destroying a strong one.[16] The information-sharing role of weak ties is increasingly being recognized, and self-help books are even being published to enable the interested reader to increase his or her pool of such contacts.[17]

A second beneficial effect of weak ties is increased power for those who possess a large number of them. A classic sociological study of a close-knit Italian neighborhood in North Boston found that, despite the village-like, intimate character of the residents' interaction within their neighborhood, they were unable to unite and resist the city planning office when it proposed to destroy the area for an urban renewal project.[18] This may have been because the residents possessed only strong ties and no weak ones:

> Such individuals may be difficult to organize or integrate with politically-based movements of any kind, since membership in movements or goal-oriented organizations typically results from being recruited by friends.[19]

Granovetter compares the Italians of the North End, who lacked weak ties, with the residents of Charleston, another Boston neighborhood. Though of the same socio-economic class, this latter group had more weak ties, and so were able to resist the urban renewal of their area more successfully.[20]

A final, and related, advantage of weak ties is in resource mobilization. The most recent theories of how social movements grow and succeed ascribe their success to their ability to locate and use a wide variety of resources.[21] Members of an encapsulated group with only strong ties will be limited in their fund-raising efforts to the amount of money they can raise among themselves; a group with a large number of weak ties may elicit smaller individual donations, but the greater pool of potential donors will result in a larger overall sum. Information, too, is a resource, and it has already been shown that weak ties are more effective at receiving and spreading information. Through weak ties, local activists are more likely to have access to skilled leaders, or to persons who have an "in" with the local government, than if they were confined only to their own intimates.

WOMEN AND WEAK TIES

The original research on weak ties investigated only those of men. Recently, however, several researchers have pointed out that the pattern of weak ties may differ for women in several important ways.[22]

Association Size

While small associations might seem preferable for getting to know one's fellow members well, large ones are better for the development of the kind of weak ties that empower participants. Large associations make a larger number of persons available for contact by the individual member, through membership lists, newsletters, and the like. Larger associations are more likely to command the attention of the media when they want it, and are more often "central" rather than "peripheral" in their influence on the larger society. Finally, of course, a large association will have more resources for its members to draw upon: more money, personnel, copying machines, expertise, and the like.

Women, however, are less likely to belong to large associations. One 1977 study of 1,800 adults in the midwest found that the male respondents' voluntary organizations averaged three times the size of those to which the women belonged.[23] The largest differences were in fraternal/sororal groups and in all types of business-related groups (both of which were four times larger for men than for women). Even the labor unions to which the men belonged were twice the size of the largely female unions.

Center/Periphery

Some associations are involved with the "center" of society —that is, they interact with those institutions that play a major role in shaping the overall direction of large-scale societal events.[24] Others—local PTAs, bridge clubs, and the like—are "peripheral," and have little or no influence beyond their own immediate members. Men tend to be members of economically-oriented central associations, and women of domestically-oriented ones on the periphery.[25] Thus, men are three times more likely than women to belong to "central" associations like business organizations, and six times more likely to belong to labor unions. Both men and women are equally likely to be members of fraternal/sororal groups, but, as has already been pointed out, the men's associations in this category are four times as large as the women's.

The result of these patterns is that women are disadvantaged, when compared to men, in the number of weak ties they can draw upon. "Overall, men are exposed to over 600 potential contacts through their average 1.69 [association] memberships, while women are exposed to fewer than 185 such contacts in their 1.61 memberships."[26]

CONCLUSIONS

Weak ties, the kind most often developed through large associations, are therefore more important than either sociologists or the general public had previously thought. Weak secondary ties do not substitute for strong primary ones—human beings will always need the affection, emotional security and help in times of crisis that strong ties provide. But weak ties confer their own unique set of benefits. Our weak ties enable us to maintain contact with a wider span of information sources than we would otherwise have access to. Weak ties empower groups, increasing their resources of money, leadership skills and contacts with potentially powerful actors. In their own way, too, weak ties effect social cohesion and a sense of community in groups that are too large to maintain communitarian ties. The annual meetings of professional associations are a good example of this latter function of weak ties: "Information and ideas flow more easily through the specialty, giving it a 'sense of community,' activated at meetings and conventions. *Maintenance of weak ties may well be the most important consequence of such meetings.*"[27] [italics mine] With these characteristics of "associational" weak ties in mind, we turn now to a consideration of the way this model might apply to religious congregations.

Associations and Religious Life

For many congregations, the associational form is now the predominant model upon which their community life is based. As many as fifty to sixty percent of the active religious in some of these congregations are living singly or in pairs, and come together with a larger group of their fellow members only periodically for prayer or discussion meetings. Whereas intentional communities of religious have to adhere to geographical limitations in order to preserve their unity, and to restrict their members to a particular diocese or a given set of schools or hospitals, an associational order might now be thinly scattered nationwide. By no stretch of the imagination can these congregations any longer be called intentional communities. And yet, as associations, they still retain some elements from their communitarian past, mixed as well with bureaucratic practices. The resulting amalgam does not always fit together satisfactorily. And the associational model, when applied to religious life, is not a perfect one. This section will consider the strengths and weaknesses of the associational model, and then outline some of the areas where it conflicts with the communitarian and bureaucratic models.

STRENGTHS OF THE ASSOCIATIONAL MODEL FOR RELIGIOUS LIFE

The strengths of associational weak ties can be especially beneficial for members of religious communities. Women religious, for example, may not be aware that they possess the oldest and most widespread network of "bridging" weak ties of any group of women in the United States—a network whose extent stuns the few feminist scholars who are aware of its existence.[28] It would be interesting to see how Milgram's "Small World" experiments would work with sisters—many might find that they either knew a member of their own community, or else knew a sister in another congregation who knew a member of her community, in almost every major city in the United States and in several European countries. These ties can be readily activated when a sister needs a place to stay during professional meetings, or when one is changing jobs and needs to scout out living possibilities in a strange city. The network also provides its members with information about what is going on in communities throughout the country. This is a tremendously empowering resource, and one that did not exist to as wide an extent when religious congregations were more encapsulated as intentional communities. While some communication and information-sharing had always existed among the leadership of pre-Vatican II congregations,[29] the rank and file usually did not have access to it. Not only were the members of one's own community more narrowly concentrated in a few locations than they are today, but the average religious was more isolated from contacts with members of other orders. Thus, prior to the late 1960s, the empowering effects of weak ties were much less available to the majority of religious in the United States.

While the information sharing characteristic of weak ties is especially important for women religious, it benefits religious of both genders. Networks based on congregational affiliation form an additional set of weak ties, in addition to the professional networks arising from their ministerial linkages. A third network may even be created, combining and integrating the first two. For example, colleges and hospitals sponsored by several different religious congregations have formed their own associations to advance their interests.[30]

In addition to information sharing, weak ties also help the members of religious communities to gain power as a group. Whereas in former times congregations had access to power because they provided key services within the church and in society, this is less true today. Many of the institutions formerly run by religious now employ far more lay persons in administrative capacities (if, indeed, they employ any religious at all), and they may even have been formally removed from the order's effective control. Furthermore, with only a minority of Catholic youth attending parochial schools, and with the development of the modern American health care system, an order's educational and health-care institutions may not seem as necessary, either to the laity or to the hierarchy, as they once did. In place of power stemming from the provision of valued resources, the associational model enables congregations to substitute the power based on organizing and tapping weak ties. The Leadership Conference of Women Religious, for example, has several times served as an information clearing house and a coordinator of response in controversies between some of the member communities and elements of the church hierarchy.

Associational ties may actually be the preferred form of organization in some situations. Granovetter cites a study of a hospital staff whose organization by weak ties was actually more efficient and led to higher morale than if the employees had been organized bureaucratically. Hospital staffs are usually integrated through strong hierarchical ties, or else an attempt is made to cultivate an artificial "family atmosphere." But both of these types of interpersonal ties were less effective: the bureaucratic ties because they were impersonal and institutional, and the communitarian "family type" ties because the group was too large for such a model.[31] With weak ties serving as bridges between smaller task groups that were more intimately connected within themselves, a level of morale and cohesion was achieved that had been impossible under the other two models. It would be interesting to see if this were similarly applicable to religious life—if small primary groups of four to eight religious could be made to substitute for the familial attachment of the intentional community, while weak ties could be used to join the sub-groups within the larger congregation.

WEAKNESSES OF THE ASSOCIATIONAL MODEL FOR RELIGIOUS LIFE

Emotional Security and Intimacy

A primary weakness of associational weak ties is that, while they do provide some sense of cohesion and camaraderie, they were never designed to provide the intimacy and emotional security that strong ties (such as those deliberately fostered in intentional communities) can provide. Members of associational religious communities, if they wish to remain psychologically healthy, will have to meet their intimacy and security needs elsewhere. Some may find an alternate community in their work setting; others may redevelop strong ties to their biological families. Still others may cling to one or two close friends within the larger congregation, often living with them in extremely stable twosomes or threesomes.[32] This results in much less member movement within a congregation than had been the case in its intentional community phase, when members were often deliberately rotated. In one typical order, for example, the average yearly turnover in its local houses during the early 1960s was over thirty percent, and few sisters remained on the same mission longer than six or seven years. Today, in that same order, over half of the active membership have been living in the same situation for at least five years.[33] This stability of living arrangements results in less flexibility for the congregation as a whole and in a more tenuous commitment to a given ministry. The leadership may not be able to persuade other members to begin working in a particular institution, if the religious currently working there have been doing so for an extended length of time. Without regular turnover of personnel, the order's commitment to a given institution becomes dependent on a few particular individuals, and may dissolve quite rapidly should these individuals become ill or retire. Placing novices in congenial living arrangements also becomes difficult when the majority of the members of a congregation have been living in the same dyads for many years. In addition to increased organizational inflexibility, paradoxically, the association model can also lead to less individual freedom; the members of a stable dyad may feel they can accept ministerial placements only in areas where both can find work, and the three or four religious who have staffed (e.g.) the same grade school for twenty years may not feel they can leave because "No one will come to take our place." This latter situation becomes a vicious circle, for it is true that no new religious will come. They would not dare to join such a long-lasting local group. If the associational form does not provide its members with the security and intimacy they need within the larger community, therefore, the individual members may create alternatives that hamper the effectiveness both of the congregation as a whole and even, sometimes, of the individuals involved.

The failure of associational weak ties to provide the intimacy of strong ties also has implications for the recruitment of new members. As long as religious congregations retain that intentional community element which bars marriage to its members, potential entrants may be reluctant to commit themselves to a group which demands the renunciation of this strong intimate tie and yet does not provide a substitute for it. This may be why the lay associate programs of many orders are growing while novitiates are not, or why, in some women's communities, more older widows and divorcees enter than young persons.

Counter-Cultural Witness

Another weakness of associations, when used as a model for religious life, is that associational congregations are less able to provide the counter-cultural witness that had been implied by their founding charisms. "For any non-profit volunteer organiza-tion to achieve any corrective or prophetic effect on American society is extremely complex and difficult."[34] The associational model, like the bureaucratic one, does not authorize a congrega-tion's leadership to challenge the members to a counter-cultural stance; only the leadership role of an intentional community in-cludes this element. Since the members of an association are also not as isolated from surrounding cultural influences as intentional community members are, they will gradually become more and more like that culture in their beliefs, values and lifestyle. It is possible, of course, to retain some willingness to challenge the mainstream culture on one aspect or another (witness the peace activists who belong to several pacifist organizations, as men-tioned earlier). Similarly, associational religious, by remaining active at their order's meetings and on its committees, may keep many key aspects of their founder's charism alive. But unless an association moves back closer to the communitarian model, the overall lifestyle of its members may become largely indistinguish-able from that of the society at large. As one critic wrote, when analyzing the renewal efforts of a congregation in the late 1960s:

> What was once a quasi-monastic women's order became a Catholic middle class voluntary association composed mainly of professional women.[35]

Religious may disagree with this assessment, arguing that they still do retain the counter-cultural aspects of their founding char-isms, and that they can even extend these aspects more readily under the associational model. It is true that the associational character of many present-day congregations does allow for the more effective mobilization of their combined resources, and that this mobilization might be directed toward counter-cultural ends. It is also true that there are other cultures in the United States, or in any society, besides that of the white middle class majority, and that the associational form would permit minority religious to adhere more closely to (e.g.) a black or Latino or working class culture than had been possible in communitarian congregations. But sociological studies of other intentional communities which later became associations, as well as some recent research on the general public's perception of modern religious, indicate that associational religious congregations are not perceived as counter-cultural, nor are they likely to become so.[36]

The emerging model of associational religious life thus appears to contain aspects that do not "mix well" with the remnants of communitarian and bureaucratic commitment which many orders still retain. The resulting interactions and adaptations have, at times, led to consequences which the members did not foresee, and which they might not have chosen if they had. The following section of this chapter will analyze some key areas of contrast between the three forms.

ASSOCIATION, BUREAUCRACY, COMMUNITY: AREAS OF CONTRAST

Levels of Involvement

An essential difference between the association model and either of the other two forms is that associations allow for different, and *personally chosen*, degrees of member involvement with the larger group. Some members of an association simply pay their dues and read the newsletter, others also attend the local meetings, and still others participate actively on both the local and national levels. In an intentional community, by contrast, all members are expected to grant to the community extensive control over most of the aspects of their lives. Intentional communities usually do not permit variations in commitment. While different degrees of involvement are possible in a bureaucracy, it is the organization that codifies these degrees and assigns them to the individual, who must comply if he or she wishes to retain membership. Association members with differing levels of involvement will have different stakes in the policies (and even in the very existence) of the organization.

In a religious community which has moved toward the associational model, this situation is further complicated by the remnants of its intentional community state, in which a high level of commitment was assumed. The ability of the associational congregation to count on such commitment and cooperation from its members will have been weakened. This situation may depart so far from the communitarian idea, and be so threatening for both the leadership and the members, that both may avoid facing it altogether. Both the leadership and the rank and file may collude in the "stage management" of certain situations so that the "performance" illusion in which each has a vested interest—in this case, that the ideology of the community is accepted and actively followed by the membership—may not be destroyed. Leaders may be reluctant to place themselves in the position of calling for any united action on the part of the membership, such as a reduction of local house expenses in order to send the surplus to the poor, or the tithing members' time in a given cause. Instead, poverty monies will be donated out of the central fund, and vague and ambiguous exhortations will be made urging the membership to do whatever they feel they can. In either case, all involved are spared the necessity of admitting that the congregation's leaders no longer possess the right to require any concrete action of the membership. This is similar to the impression management practiced by "teams" or groups of interacting persons, as Erving Goffman observed:

> It seems to be generally felt that public disagreement among the members of a team not only incapacitates them for united action but also embarrasses the reality sponsored by the team. To protect the impression of reality, members of the team may be required to postpone taking public stands until the position of the team has been settled. . . . Whatever the number of teams, there will be a sense in which the interaction can

be analyzed in terms of the co-operative effort of all participants to maintain a working consensus.[37]

The association model, therefore, joins with the bureaucratic
one in challenging the right possessed by communitarian leaders
of exercising spiritual leadership. But it goes further. Even the
right to oversee finances and ministerial placement, which both
the bureaucratic and communitarian models grant to leadership, is
challenged by the association model.

Financial Considerations

In an association, members are financially independent of the
larger group to a much greater extent than is possible in either a
bureaucracy or an intentional community. An association, in fact,
has no right to its members' money, beyond their fixed annual
dues and any voluntary contributions they may choose to add.
When a more associational congregation's members are dispersed
in areas with widely differing costs of living, it may become
necessary for them to manage their own finances, independently
of congregational guidelines. Many communities have members
who keep separate bank accounts, instead of turning over—or,
sometimes, even reporting—their incomes to the congregation.
Since this arrangement is more compatible with the association
model, it can be expected to become more common in the future.
Such a shift in the locus of financial control often results in a
corresponding power shift: a study of one community found that,
once the congregation depended on the individual members for
financial support, instead of the individual members depending on
the congregation, the order lost its power over the individual. The
only sanction possible in instances of member transgression was
to drop the offending individual from the membership rolls, or to
deny him/her access to educational and spiritual functions—neither of which was very effective: "There was little indication
that the central administration could command anyone to do
anything."[38]

Changing financial arrangements may also have legal ramifications, both civil and canonical. Congregations may lose their tax-exempt status, and different Social Security regulations may apply to members than had applied before. If an order totally adopts the associational model, removing the requirement for celibacy, the vow of poverty would have to be reevaluated in the light of providing for members' children. Another possible model would be to allow associational commitment, with its financial independence and the possibility of marriage, for the membership at large, and retain a more communitarian format in the central core.[39] In this case, the respective responsibilities, financial and otherwise, of each of the two levels of commitment would have to be carefully worked out.

As long as a congregation retains elements from its former state as an intentional community, it will experience some areas of confusion and dissonance between communitarian requirements and those of associations. The response of many, if not most, orders to this situation is to avoid dealing with it. Previous attempts by social researchers to raise the issue for discussion have been ignored or even actively resisted, as Arbuckle points out.[40] Such avoidance, however, does not resolve the contradictions which exist between the commitment levels implied by a congregation's associational, bureaucratic and communitarian aspects. And the longer the contradictions are allowed to persist without being faced, the more amorphous the membership expectations are likely to become. This is not good for the continuing existence of the congregation—under any model.

Conclusion

Can the associational model—or some permutation of it with communitarian and bureaucratic elements—become the new paradigm for religious life? Previous sociological research has not been optimistic about the possibility. Several studies of nineteenth century intentional communities, for example, found that many of them did ultimately move to a looser, more associational form of commitment. *But none of the ones which did so lasted beyond a single generation.*[41] Despite the numerous authors who have lamented the suppression of the Beguines or the monasticization of groups such as the Ursulines and the Dominicans,[42] it may be that only those orders which conform themselves—voluntarily or involuntarily—to the intentional community model can hope to survive.

This is not a pleasant observation to make, especially if the research ascribing psychologically- and spiritually-detrimental effects to the commitment mechanisms of intentional communities is also true. Religious life may at times appear to be trapped between the Scylla of a psychologically-destructive intentional community which tends to become an end in itself, and the Charybdis of an ultimately unstable and gradually co-opted association. An increased familiarity with the sociological studies of other groups which have tried similar commitment model changes may make it possible to design techniques by which an associational-bureaucratic-communitarian amalgam can avoid the pitfalls inherent in any one of the models alone. Questions vital to a religious congregation's survival, such as how to recruit members effectively, and whether or not to invest the community's energy and resources in ministerial institutions, could be explored using each model, and plans of action might be devised that incorporate the benefits of all three. The following chapters will sketch some tentative directions which could be explored.

5

Recruiting and Retaining
Group Members

Whether or not its members acknowledge or are even aware of it, the single most vital issue that any group faces is the retention of its current members and the recruitment of new ones. Without an assured supply of quality personnel, a group will decline and eventually die. Membership growth is so important that it often eclipses the original goal(s) which the organization was created to achieve. Sociological literature is filled with accounts of how businesses and government agencies have neglected product development or service delivery, and, instead, have become preoccupied with acquiring other companies or with squabbling over the funding increases needed to survive and expand.[1]

Religious congregations, with their declining or non-existent entrance rates and their rising median ages, are facing organizational death. The total number of women religious in the United States, which had risen over twenty-three percent between 1950 and 1966 (from 147,000 to 181,421), has since fallen forty percent and stands at under 105,000. The median age of women religious is sixty-six; thirty-nine percent are over seventy years old.[2] The number of Jesuits, the largest male religious order, fell from 35,038 worldwide in 1965 to 24,924 in 1988. "In the U.S., the society lost 195 Jesuits through deaths and departures in 1987 alone."[3] Worldwide, some 100,000 religious have left their orders.[4] In addition to the loss of their current members, the number of new entrants to both male and female religious congregations has fallen seventy-five percent in the past twenty years.[5] This decline has occurred at the precise time when one would have expected the post-war Baby Boom to supply an even larger number of entrants than usual.[6]

Religious congregations have taken surprisingly few actions to reverse their decline. This is organizationally unusual, for bureaucracies and voluntary associations typically respond to such situations by concerted or even frantic attempts at damage control. At times, some organizations go so far as to change their basic purpose or focus, if their old one is no longer viable. Religious communities, in contrast, appear to be accepting their demise rather passively. This may be due to several reasons. Arbuckle and Markham suggest that massive denial is at work.[7] Alternatively, the decline may seem so extensive as to be irreversible; consequently, members of religious communities may assume that nothing can, or should, be done. A third possibility, the one which will be addressed in this chapter, is that the recruitment and retention requirements of bureaucracies, associations and intentional communities differ to such an extent that they set up competing and contradictory agendas both for vocation personnel and for the orders as a whole. The recruitment strategies appropriate to the intentional communities that religious congregations once were are no longer acceptable in their new, more associational present. At the same time, however, many congregations retain enough of these communitarian expectations to deter potential entrants who are looking for associational membership. And several bureaucratic admission standards may also have been adopted, without critically examining how these standards might affect either associational or communitarian recruitment.

In order to analyze the relative merits of the recruitment and retention strategies appropriate to religious congregations as bureaucracies and as voluntary associations, it is first necessary to explore what needs were served by the traditional vocation practices of their communitarian past. The following section will outline the basic recruitment and socialization techniques which all successful intentional communities have had to employ in order to attract new members and to awaken in them a strong commitment to the community's world view. The problems of generational change and the gradual waning of member enthusiasm will be considered as possible reasons for the eventual failure of recruitment strategies in intentional communities. These findings will then be compared with the preconditions for successful recruitment to associations, and an assessment will be made of how well religious congregations meet these preconditions.

Recruitment and Retention in Intentional Communities

THE IMPLICATIONS OF COMMUNAL COMMITMENT

In chapter 2 it was emphasized that intense ideological and cathetic commitment are needed in an intentional community. Only then will its members be motivated to subordinate their individual needs and desires to those of the larger group. The need to develop and maintain this commitment in new members has several implications for the kind of recruitment and socialization strategies which all intentional communities must follow.

Targeting and Resocializing Youth

Intentional communities must, by and large, draw their new members from comparatively youthful age cohorts. Previous studies of communal groups have found that the average recruit was between the ages of twenty and thirty—very few were over forty years old when they entered.[8] This pattern occurs for several reasons. First of all, an intentional community's demands for communal togetherness and boundary maintenance mean that new entrants should have few competing affectional ties to draw them away from the group. Young people are less likely to have these ties: they are not yet married and have no children, for example.[9] Often they may also be newly-arrived at a university or in a strange city to begin a new job, and thus may have few friendship ties.[10] This comparative affectional isolation means that some young people are particularly open to developing ties of friendship with members of the communal group. Certain cults such as the Unification Church, for example, have deliberately exploited this openness to attract their members.

Of course, there are other categories of people who are comparatively lacking in affectional ties. Widows with grown and absent children, for example, are sometimes targeted for recruitment by religious cults. But there is a second reason for recruiting youths instead of older widows. This is the ideological commitment which an intentional community demands of its members. The young are more intellectually malleable. In his famous essay on "The Problem of Generations," Karl Mannheim contends that an individual's "personal experimentation with life" begins between the ages of 17 and 21.[11] At this time, the young person personally chooses a set of values and beliefs from among those which are offered by various cultural elements within the society. After this choice, an individual's opinions are much more fixed. It is harder for an older adult to change and adopt the world view of a communal group, especially if that world view is sharply different from the beliefs of the mainstream culture. For this reason, older persons are more likely to be pressured to give their money to an intentional community than to join it.

Even though it is easier to resocialize young people than older adults to ideological commitment, such resocialization still requires profoundly intrusive practices and techniques. The process, Ewens states, is similar to

> ... the putting off of the old self and the taking on of a new mode of life in such institutions as prisons, mental hospitals and communist "re-education" camps. [There are] similar-

ities between the techniques used in these institutions and those used in convents, particularly novitiates. Removal from one's former world and support system, total dependence on those in charge, and control of all communication—including those non-verbal and verbal messages that help us define who we are—are part of the complicated process.[12]

This process has usually been looked upon negatively by historians of pre-Vatican II religious life—and, indeed, it is quite destructive psychologically. *But only through such techniques have intentional communities typically been able to elicit the ideological commitment they need from new members,* especially after the charismatic founder is no longer present. Successful intentional communities, therefore, have usually confined their recruiting to young adults, and have intensively resocialized their new members to adopt the group's world view. As the following section will explain, however, these recruitment practices, while necessary in the short term, eventually expose an intentional community to difficulties as its members approach succeeding generations of young people with their message.

Generational Change and Recruitment to Intentional Communities

In sociological literature, a generation is more than simply a result of biological—or even psychological—age. Socially, the members of one generation differ from the next because they experience a given set of events at a particular moment of their lives. Living through the Great Depression, or the change from the Latin to the English Mass, had a different impact on children of eight than on adults of fifty. And, of course, for those born after a given event, the emotions and issues which accompanied it were not part of their life experiences at all.[13] When members of a given generational cohort reach young adulthood, they are confronted by the deficiencies and distortions which are endemic to their surrounding culture—deficiencies and distortions that had arisen in previous eras and in reaction to needs which the younger generation does not remember:

> The young adults of the immediate post-Vatican II period, whose own childhood faith had been shaped by rote-memorized catechism questions and a vaguely understood Latin Mass, now confront a new generation who have had neither of these experiences. Whereas the former group's background has acutely sensitized them to the dangers of mechanical ritual and rigid doctrine, the amorphous religious instruction and "Low Church" Masses which the latter group experienced in *their* youth have left some of them with a hunger for theological absolutes and the mystery of ritual that may forever be incomprehensible to the 1960's generation.[14]

Thus, generations often alternate between opposing poles—liberalism and conservatism in politics, for example, or realism and romanticism in literature. The length of these alternating periods depends on the pace of change in the larger society.

Intentional communities have always had to deal with the problem of generational changes, both internally and externally. Communes such as the Israeli kibbutzim, which are composed of married couples, must deal with the "Sabra phenomenon," whereby the children of the founding members, after growing up in the environment which their parents had deliberately created and chosen as adults, have an entirely different attitude toward their own membership in it.[15] Celibate groups such as religious congregations, which do not have to deal with the members' children as potential entrants, nevertheless have to contend with the fact that generations are changing in the world around them. What may have been a comparatively easy transition to religious life from a pre-industrial, rural environment may be much more stressful for post-industrial, urban youth. As the community's world view and customs diverge from the culture of its potential recruits, more and more intrusive resocializing techniques must be employed to remold the new members, with all the psychological trauma—and eventual failure—that this implies. The surrounding environment appears today to be changing at a more rapid rate, which makes all communal religious groups less able to maintain long-term stability today than in former decades.[16]

An intentional community cannot have more than one genera-
tional interpretation of its founding world view current among its
members at the same time. Since a communal group makes strin-
gent demands upon the freedom of its individual members, it is
vital that the individual not mistrust the vision of those whose job
it is to implement community decisions. The members of different generations generally focus on different dangers and opportunities, and so each age group will always fear that the others are
making a terrible mistake by embarking on this or that perilous
course. ("Don't they remember what happened in the bad old days
when we used to do that?" No, they don't—they weren't around
then. "Don't they see how terribly lacking the current policy is?"
No, they can't—they're preoccupied with avoiding the dangers
they saw in their own youth.) Despite the psychologically detrimental effects of resocializing new members out of their generationally-influenced attitudes and opinions, most intentional communities have not been able to avoid doing so, because retaining
different generational attitudes will lead them to schism or dissolution.

Generational Change in Religious Life

Recently, many religious congregations have revised their
initial formation programs so that they are less damaging to new
members. However desirable this may be from a psychological
standpoint, it has meant that generational differences have not
been smoothed over as they had been in the past. This is extremely important, because young adults today have no memory
of the pre-Vatican II church. As a new member of one congregation said to her novice director: "Vatican II, Vatican II, that's all
you talk about—like it happened yesterday." Without a personal
experience of the pre-Vatican II church, today's young people
(which, in this context, means anyone under the age of thirty-five)
will not be able to see or appreciate the deficiencies of that era—
however obvious these deficiencies may appear to age cohorts
only ten years their senior. And older religious may never truly
understand what it was like to grow up with totally amorphous

doctrinal instruction, to remember, as one thirty-four year old brother does of his twelve years of parochial school religious education, only that he "made a lot of collages."

Many young Catholics reacted to their childhood experiences by discounting even nominal church membership as having any relevance in their lives. Others sought in religious life the structure and stability they had missed earlier—evidence is surfacing, for example, that young priests and seminarians today are much more conservative than the generation that preceded them. "The widely-discussed conservatism and clericalism among Catholic seminarians in the 1980's is clearly visible. The priests 26–35 years old in 1985 were no more liberal than those 36–45, often less so; they were more doctrinally orthodox and less socially involved than priests of the same age in 1970."[17]

Recall that the members of an intentional community are extremely threatened by the possibility that their fellow members may have a different interpretation of the founding ideology than they do. *In no intentional community is authority ever peacefully transferred from the followers of one generational interpretation to the followers of another.* To the extent that religious congregations still retain elements of their past as intentional communities, they, too, will resist admitting persons of obviously different (and usually more conservative) views. Often these views will be interpreted as an indication of a basic immaturity that renders the candidate unfit for religious life:

> Recruits with this [conservative fundamentalist] background also ought to be screened. If they need a strict discipline or the perks and garbs of priesthood, their motivation may be more personal than what is generally good for Church ministry and religious orders.[18]

But psychological immaturity is not the same as having a generationally-influenced world view. The young recruit described in the preceding quote may indeed be immature, but so would a novice of the 1960s who wanted to move immediately into ghetto ministry and neglected to develop his or her prayer life. Every generational world view also has its aspects of immaturity. The danger arises when the gatekeepers to a religious congregation mistake the former for the latter.

Of course, it must be admitted that most religious congregations are not beseiged by hordes of young people begging to be allowed to enter, don a habit, and follow a strict horarium, even if the congregations had been disposed to admit them. Modern religious congregations, by initiating the very renewal and updating called for by Vatican II, may have made themselves unattractive ("not holy enough") to the one group of young people still seeking to enter, whether or not these young people are correct in feeling this way. More liberal youth are less attracted to religion in general, and to religious life in particular: one study of religious and diocesan priests indicates that those who espoused liberal views on clergy political activism or the role of women were the least likely to enter the seminary in the first place, and the most likely to leave.[19]

The contrasting foci of the older and the younger generations' world views may not only be the reason why few young people enter a congregation, it may also be the reason why the present members can face this dearth of recruits with equanimity —intentional communities often prefer even death to the usurpation of their ideological world view by followers of another perspective. The acceptance of organizational extinction, which is so atypical of bureaucracies and associations, may be due to the fact that their lingering communitarian past renders religious reluctant to yield control over their founding ideology to a new generation.[20]

Conclusions

The findings of the various sociological studies on intentional communities, therefore, indicate that such groups must preserve their members' ideological commitment in order both to survive and to attract new entrants. This necessity has generally meant that communal groups must recruit members at a young age and resocialize them extensively. But that task becomes harder and harder over the years, as changes in the surrounding culture lead to new generational orientations in potential entrants. On the other hand, failure to resocialize members out of their generational differences will lead to tension and even schism, as each age cohort vies with the other over control of the group's direction. As a consequence, many intentional communities—including religious congregations, to the extent that they retain elements of their communitarian past—screen out applicants who exhibit signs of different perspectives. They follow this procedure even if it means organizational death, for nothing is more threatening to members of an intentional community than the possibility that they may have committed their future to followers of an ideology discrepant from their own. A basic factor in the failure of vocation programs in religious life may therefore be that congregations still retain communitarian expectations of ideological conformity but have discarded the resocialization mechanisms that are needed to achieve it.

Recruitment and Retention in Associations

Perhaps religious congregations should therefore give more attention to the recruitment requirements of associational groups, and to the techniques that have proven successful in attracting members to these types of organizations. As a recent writer on the subject suggested:

> If we are to attract more vocations to women's communities, it may be necessary to arrive at new legislation that clarifies and more accurately reflects their living situation. Perhaps women should be given the opportunity to form associations more similar to the diocesan priesthood—associations which envision living alone, and having responsibility for one's own funds, receiving trust and support in their work, health insurance, etc. These new forms of the apostolate will reach at times beyond individual parishes or dioceses—like the move-

ments for peace and a just economy and, for example, soup kitchens and pantries, shelters for homeless people, and training of liturgical ministers. Or the sisters might be placed in charge of parishes or specific ministries within the parish, directly under the bishops as diocesan priests are.[21]

What Stuhlmueller is advocating here is that religious congregations acknowledge openly what they have de facto become: associational, voluntary groups instead of intentional communities. If this is done, he implies, they will be better able to attract new vocations.

But is this necessarily true? Associations have their own requirements for successful recruitment strategies, which must be taken into account if they wish to attract new members. The following section will outline some of these requirements, and will point out how seldom they have been fulfilled in religious life.

PRECONDITIONS FOR ASSOCIATIONAL GROWTH

Previous research on associations has indicated that they will grow and increase in size only if certain key preconditions are met.[22] First of all, there have to be many potential members who are available for recruitment. Labor unions, for example, can become large because they are open to all the workers in a certain industry or occupation nationwide. By contrast, a PTA or neighborhood association is limited to the parents of a particular group of school children or the residents of a particular area. A second precondition is that there must exist strong political or economic reasons for the organization to be large. To refer to the labor union example again, the more members the union can attract, the greater bargaining power it will have. Thus, its current members will have a strong incentive actively to recruit their fellow workers. Third, a high percentage of the potential membership pool must in fact become members. This is more likely if there is an economic incentive for doing so, such as the higher wages available to union members, or the increased professional contacts and referrals available through a professional association. The fourth precondition is that potential members cannot have so many other demands on their time or mobility that they are unable to take on the competing commitment of belonging to, and becoming active in, the association.

How do religious congregations, when considered as associations, measure up under these criteria? There are, it is true, many potential members who could be targeted for recruitment. As the Baby Boom generation passed through young adulthood in the 1970s and early 1980s, an unprecedented number of young Catholics was available for membership. Did religious congregations have strong economic or political reasons to approach them? *Very possibly they did not.* It could be argued that religious congregations already had as much power vis-à-vis the hierarchical church as they were likely to get in the foreseeable future, and that, especially for women religious, this was not a very significant amount. It was unlikely that adding another hundred, or even another thousand, members would give them any additional political leverage in the church. Furthermore, women in religious congregations, as they became more aware of their powerlessness, may even have been reluctant to encourage others to submit to such restrictions:

> Families do not welcome guests during times of internal crises, nor do they feel at ease welcoming the prospective spouses of their members at such times. So, too, it has been difficult for many religious women to encourage candidates when they themselves feel somewhat under siege. Likewise, the very tenuousness of a time of transition does not create a good climate for the induction of new members.[23]

Few of the members of religious congregations were motivated during the 1970s and 1980s to approach potential entrants and invite them to join. Thus, the second precondition for an association's growth has been lacking. The third precondition for growth is that outsiders see and value the benefits of belonging to the group. Today, potential members experience few incentives to enter religious life. Alternatives exist for those who are interested in church and charitable service, "alternatives less permanent, less confining, less entangled in recondite canonical legalities" than religious life.[24] Religious life seems to offer no advantages that lay service does not also offer, and, in fact, is burdened with some profound liabilities. For example, the increasingly monogenerational character of religious congregations is a deterrent:

> Does the woman of 25 or 26 want to accept responsibility for a future with women whose median age is between 55 and 65? Is she willing to do this without a strong peer group?[25]

Additionally, recent research on the attitudes of young lay women toward women religious indicates that they are not very positive. And, in one study, the younger the lay respondent, the less attractive an image of women religious she held.[26] Another study, a 1987 survey of over three thousand female high school students conducted in the Newark archdiocese, elicited over one hundred suggestions from the respondents on how to encourage vocations. Almost twenty percent of these suggestions stressed negative stereotypes of sisters and the need to promote a more positive image of their life:

> —Stereotyped images of sisters need to be changed. Stories of parents about sisters make them sound inhuman. Positive side of religious life needs to be stressed.
> —Educate the public about different facets of religious life so stereotypical images are removed.
> —Shatter stereotypes. Develop awareness of religious women as intelligent, dynamic, committed . . .
> —Make religious life more pleasing and exciting and not such a "dead end."[27]

Another set of responses to the same survey, accounting for seventeen of the total of one hundred and five, emphasized the "second class" status of women in the church as a deterrent to religious vocations. While the study did not survey the opinions of young males, there is no reason to believe that they would be much different. Under these conditions, it is highly unlikely that young people—especially young females—would see any advantage in joining associational religious life.

The fourth precondition for an association's growth is that the potential members not have competing commitments that interfere with their ability to participate in the group. In this respect, religious communities are particularly disadvantaged. Because they were formerly intentional communities, religious congregations still require a much stronger commitment for full membership than other associations do, notably permanent celibacy and the surrender of control over one's personal wealth. Such a level of commitment is a lot to expect from potential recruits, especially when a religious congregation is perceived as being able to offer them so little in return.

Could this dilemma be resolved by abandoning celibacy, communal finances, and permanent commitment as requirements for full membership? Some religious communities have made tentative steps in this direction by admitting associate members, many of whom are married, and all of whom manage their own finances separately from the congregation. A few writers have argued that this is the new form of religious life for the twenty-first century. Such a change would, indeed, address the fourth precondition for growth. But so loosening the demands of membership is likely to attract sufficient new members *only if the second and third preconditions can somehow also be fixed.* This means that religious congregations have to figure out a way to offer something that lay service in the church cannot, and also (for women's religious congregations at least) to counteract the weak and negative reputation that they have among young lay women.

These liabilities are severe ones, and probably explain why previously studied intentional communities that moved toward an associational model did not survive.[28]

COMPETING RECRUITMENT STRATEGIES: SUCCESS AND FAILURE

Religious congregations' current recruiting strategies, therefore, meet the needs of neither their communitarian past nor their more associational present. Furthermore, the sometimes half-hearted attempts to follow recruitment strategies appropriate to one of these two models actually hinders the successful use of the tactics necessary for the other. Finally, several bureaucratically-influenced practices have been added, which also affect both the communitarian and the associational procedures. The remainder of this chapter will first outline the specific factors—both internally and in the surrounding environment—which have helped or hindered religious congregations in attracting new members. Suggestions will be made for how religious orders, whether predominantly associational or predominantly communitarian, might proceed in the future. Finally, an attempt will be made to indicate and evaluate the contributions of the bureaucratic model to the process.

Internal Factors Affecting the Recruitment Process in Communitarian Religious Congregations

The sociological studies which have been done of successful recruiting techniques among intentional communities unanimously agree that a potential recruit *must* experience personal contact with joyful and enthusiastic members who are the recruit's peers in age and background.[29] Studies of the priesthood and religious life confirm that a similar process takes place: the most important vocational influence cited by priests in a 1970 study was the personal encouragement of another priest or a nun.[30] In the past, the clergy and religious in a parish actively encouraged vocations: churches and schools in a diocese competed with each other to send the largest number of young men and women to the seminary and local motherhouses each year.[31] In the 1970 study, however, the respondents admitted that they themselves were less likely to encourage young men to join the priesthood, even while they acknowledged the importance of such encouragement in their own lives. It is vital that every member of those religious congregations which intend to remain intentional communities take personal responsibility for contacting young adults and inviting them to enter religious life.

Religious are, however, less likely today to be in a position to initiate this contact. The movement of Catholic families into suburban areas where the public school system may be much better than the parochial one (if, indeed, a Catholic school exists at all), and the withdrawal of religious from the Catholic schools that remain, has meant that fewer young people experience any interaction with a religious. As Hennessy stated, "We are not part of—or at best a relatively marginal part of—their parish life. We are seldom part of their school life. We scarcely exist for them."[32] The Newark survey of Catholic high school students mentioned a similar lack of contact in twenty-one of the suggestions offered —one-fifth of the total. "It is obvious from the responses," the study concluded, "that young women, at a time when they are considering lifestyles and careers, receive insufficient information about religious life as a viable option. Likewise, they have very little involvement with religious women as persons."[33]

But mere contact with religious is not enough. Potential entrants to an intentional community must also see joy and enthusiasm among its members. Initially, researchers have found, visible happiness is even more important for prospective members than intellectual conviction of the truth of the group's world view: if they are attracted to the community's people, recruits will be disposed to convince themselves of the truth of the community's message.[34]

According to several studies, however, many present day religious are quite lonely—in the terminology of the second chapter, they have lost cathetic commitment to their religious congregation.[35] Not only is this loneliness the strongest predictor of leaving religious life, but the dissatisfaction and depression of the lonely religious is usually visible to potential entrants, and acts as a deterrent. Some authors have also suggested that many religious have lost their ideological commitment as well. "The diminishment (perhaps, in some cases, a loss) of corporate identity by religious communities seems to me to be the most important reason for the lack of vocations."[36] Many religious are no longer sure what the reason and purpose of religious life is in today's world. "This ambiguity seems to exist in spite of the presence of well-documented and articulated mission statements."[37] After two decades without any substitute for their former commitment mechanisms, and with the rise of alternate associational models of commitment, many religious appear trapped between the two, experiencing profound ideological and cathetic alienation. Such members will hardly be attractive to new recruits considering either model of religious life.

Successful recruiting strategies for intentional communities also use recruiters who are similar in age and background to the target population. Obviously, few such persons are available in many religious congregations. Even the few young people who do enter may be put off by the top-heavy age structure of the group and hesitate to invite their peers to join. For example, the tendency of religious to spend congregational gatherings by telling stories of the old days may be perceived as excluding the few young members present who have not experienced these events. When a congregation was more multi-generational, there was less likelihood that one age group could so monopolize social conversation.

An alternate source of members for religious congregations could be older persons seeking a mid-life career or lifestyle change. Widowed or divorced parents with grown children, for example, would be free to commit themselves to religious life. They might also be less likely to be deterred by the top-heavy age structure of most religious congregations, since they themselves would be of similar age. In the coming decades, as the Baby Boom generation ages, there will also be more persons in this category than there will be in the relatively small ("Baby Bust") generation born in the 1970s. However, middle-aged recruits will probably not be amenable to the kinds of resocialization practices that a purely intentional community would have to employ. Congregations seeking to attract new members from this age category would probably have to be at least partly associational in form.

Environmental Factors Affecting the Recruitment Process in Communitarian Religious Congregations

In addition to the fact that elements internal to religious life render communitarian tactics of recruitment less effective, environmental changes in American Catholic culture have also had an impact. Citing several of these changes—the loss of permanency in modern life, for example—has become a truism in articles that consider reasons for declining vocations. This section will consider specifically how such environmental changes would impact on any intentional community's membership recruitment and retention.

An often-cited factor in the decline of religious vocations is the waning of a ghettoized Catholic culture in America, a culture which had previously rewarded and valued the choice of religious life by its young people. To point out that youth of former decades may have entered religious life partly because their parents (and they themselves) derived status from this action is not to denigrate the authenticity of their call. On the contrary, the apparent dependence of a belief or value on societal support should not be "prima facie evidence of its inauthenticity," but rather a necessary structural aid to commitment.[38] The lack of supportive cultural incentives to enter is a prime reason for the decline of any intentional community, and religious congregations cannot expect to be different in this regard. In order to survive in communitarian form, a religious community must somehow adapt itself to its changed environment, so that it is once again an attractive lifestyle option for assimilated Catholics today. This is, to say the least, a difficult task, for many aspects of modern American culture pose severe problems for the very possibility of ideological commitment and for the mechanisms needed to maintain it.

As several commentators have pointed out, the congregations founded here during the first half of the nineteenth century had attempted to adapt the European model of religious life to American culture.[39] However, "as the nineteenth century progressed, the American Catholic Church moved from standing with American culture to become less democratic and more hierarchical and to stand against American culture."[40] Reflecting this change, orders also began to conform more closely to the European model of religious life.[41] This conformity was codified in the 1917 promulgation of canon law.

Religious congregations, therefore, never really developed a set of intentional community commitment mechanisms that were congruent with American culture, but fell back instead on aspects of the old European monastic model. Initially, this may not have made much difference, since religious communities were composed either of immigrants themselves or of the children of immigrants. But as the twentieth century progressed, succeeding generations became more and more Americanized. The commitment mechanisms to which they were subjected in their resocialization process as novices exacerbated the increasing disjuncture between the American culture to which they had been assimilated and their new culture in the religious congregation.

To state that the commitment mechanisms of European monastic life do not fit well in American culture is to make the same observation that Hostie and others have made about religious life in Africa, Latin America and other areas.[42] But an added complication exists in the American case. Basic American values exist which deny the legitimacy of *any* commitment mechanisms. Contemporary American culture typically includes such values as personal fulfillment of individual talents and aspirations, self-determination and freedom from arbitrary authority, pluralism and tolerance of different world views, democratic self-criticism and freedom of speech.[43] "Its center is the autonomous individual, presumed able to choose the roles he will play and the commitments he will make, not on the basis of higher truths but according to the criteria of life effectiveness as the individual judges it."[44] Much of American culture is fundamentally opposed to the very existence of any practices that would serve to subordinate the individual to the needs of the group, as all intentional community commitment mechanisms must do. Self-deprivation is also an uncomfortable idea for most Americans: "Historically speaking, we are probably the largest culture which has ever existed devoted to the pursuit of happiness and speedy gratification."[45] Thus, to the extent that U.S. Catholics have become more like other Americans in their cultural values, they are less likely to accept the limitations that the intentional community model of religious life must of necessity impose.[46]

The decline of ghetto Catholicism has also been accompanied by a rise in the educational level of U.S. Catholics, to the point where Catholics now equal mainline Protestants in this respect.[47] In contrast, most religious prior to Vatican II were from less educated and working-class backgrounds.[48] Increased education is often associated with a greater awareness of the detrimental psychological effects of membership in intentional communities. There is a pervasive tendency, both within and outside religious life, to denounce commitment mechanisms as destructive of the individual person:

> An artificial "convent culture" which could only be maintained through brainwashing and milieu control [is] hardly the ambiance for the development of mature Christian personalities or a healthy community life.[49]

Such views among parents make it more likely that they will strongly discourage their children from entering such a damaging way of life. Research has indicated a pronounced decline in the willingness of parents to encourage their sons to become priests; similar parental reluctance with regard to daughters becoming nuns was cited in the Newark survey.[50]

Another environmental change which has impacted upon vocations is the increased alternatives available to young Catholics today. The young man of a generation ago, for whom the priesthood may have been the only avenue to upward social mobility, is now a college student anticipating a professional career. For young women, the widening of perceived options is even more striking; whether or not such options actually exist in the real world, the women believe that they do. And the limitations to the rise of women in the church are openly evident, whereas the "glass ceiling" restricting their upward mobility in the business world is often not visible to young women before they encounter it themselves in later life.

Finally, college-age women today have largely adopted the formerly male cultural belief in the necessity of sexual activity for psychological health and social happiness. A recent survey of college students found that seventy percent of the women had had sexual intercourse (including fifty-seven percent of those who said that religion was "very important" to them), as had eighty-three percent of the men. Furthermore, the women who reported having had sexual intercourse were twice as likely to say they were very satisfied with their social lives, and their life in general.[51] For all of these reasons—assimilation to mainstream American values, a greater variety of perceived opportunities, and a change in sexual mores—young people are more likely today to evaluate competing lifestyle alternatives as more attractive than religious life, and may even consider the latter as unhealthy.

Associational Recruiting Strategies

Religious congregations which shift to the associational model and focus their recruiting efforts either on married associate members or on divorced or widowed persons would also find themselves affected by changes in the larger American culture. To begin with, the increasing number of dual-earner families has meant that fewer individuals are available for active membership in *any* voluntary association. The "unemployed" housewives whose underappreciated labor made possible a host of city beautification projects, scout meetings, and Little League games are now in the paid labor force, and must strictly ration their hours of participation in extra organizations. Associational religious communities must compete with a plethora of other worthy groups for a shrinking pool of individuals with the free time to devote to them. The fourth of the preconditions for an association's growth—the availability of potential members with sufficient free time—will become more and more difficult to fulfill.

The assimilation of third and fourth generation immigrant Catholics into mainstream American culture has also affected the third precondition for associational growth—whether a specifically Catholic association will be attractive to potential members. Catholic fraternal/sororal organizations such as the Knights of Columbus, the Holy Name Society, or the Daughters of Isabella are less appealing to today's young Catholics than they were to their parents or grandparents, for the younger generation's friendship networks span a wider variety of religious and non-religious groups. In contrast, parishes earlier in the twentieth century offered such a complete round of group-based activities that it was possible for a family's entire friendship network to be composed solely of fellow parishioners.[52] An associational religious congregation must offer some unique benefit that makes joining it attractive. Based on the experience of other Catholic associations, merely offering a chance to interact with other members, or even to engage in some social service, will no longer be a sufficient drawing card to attract new members. And if an associational congregation decides to define sharing and deepening its members' prayer life as its primary goal and purpose, this may bring it into competition with other growing groups such as the Focolare or the Cursillo Movement. (Indeed, if the future of religious life lies in the associational model, these latter groups may be more successful at it than a formerly communitarian religious congregation could be.)

A variety of internal and external conditions have thus limited the ability of religious orders—both as intentional communities and as associations—to attract and recruit new members. Unless congregations can adapt to these changed circumstances in such a way as to become attractive again to young Catholics, they will die. The following section gives some recommendations on how this adaptation might be begun.

RECOMMENDATIONS

Whether a religious congregation remains an intentional community, shifts fully to the associational model, or adopts some combination of the two, the success of its vocation policies will depend on how well it can adapt them to the strengths and weaknesses of the model(s) its members have chosen. The following are some tentative recommendations for how to do this.

For Congregations That Remain Intentional Communities

A strength of the communitarian model is that it alone makes provision for the deep ideological and cathetic commitment which remains profoundly attractive to some American Catholics. Many religious still possess this commitment, and probably at an even deeper and more mature level than in the days of their dependence on pre-Vatican II commitment mechanisms. This commitment must be made visible and shared. "If religious are to attract vocations ... it will be necessary for them to be more willing to share with others the contemplative dimensions of their lives and to share that this is a priority [with them]."[53] It is difficult for most Americans to share their deepest values, since our culture holds that one's religion is an essentially subjective phenomenon which should not be imposed on others.[54] But members of communitarian religious congregations must make specific efforts to overcome this reticence. The congregation itself ought to provide ways for its members to develop their skills in expressing their foundational beliefs to outsiders. Perhaps special role-playing sessions could be held in which community members practice approaching a co-worker or a student and sharing their joy in and commitment to religious life. The newest members of the community might be asked to observe these sessions, to give feedback and to share the experience of their own invitation to the congregation.[55]

The fundamental discontinuity between American values and those of communitarian religious life must also be faced. Ideally, religious communities could hope for a "re-Catholicizing" of middle-class American Catholic youth—an increase in their knowledge of their faith (which is, as many commentators have pointed out, abysmal), and, more importantly, in their belief in and attachment to it.[56] Communities could also wait for mainstream American values to become more supportive of the sacrifices involved in intentional community commitment. In either case, however, they are likely to wait a long time. Another possibility is to locate those subcultures which may still be supportive of religious vocations and then to concentrate recruitment efforts there.

To address the issue more actively would require several steps. First of all, congregations must listen to young people to find out what they do believe and value. This involves formal, scientific research on the subject as well as more informal contact with young people in general. Such contact is necessary, not only by the formation staff to whom this task is officially delegated, but also by congregational leaders and, indeed, by every member of the community. Orders which intend to remain intentional communities must also devise commitment mechanisms which are more congruent with American culture and which, especially, take account of the objection that previous commitment mechanisms were psychologically unhealthy. This will be very difficult, because such commitment mechanisms have not been constructed before for religious congregations in our culture. Perhaps some hint of how to begin might be obtained from studying the ways the early nineteenth century congregations attempted to adjust to American life, before their reconformation to the European monastic model. The insights of both sociology and psychology would also have to be employed to design ways in which a sufficient level of group commitment could be maintained without being detrimental to the individuals in the group. In any event, without the joy and enthusiasm engendered by successful, healthy commitment mechanisms, religious congregations which are intentional communities will never attract sufficient new members to survive.

For Congregations That Have Become Associations

Since the prospect of permanent celibacy appears to be the single greatest deterrent to entering the priesthood or religious life among young people in the United States today,[57] associational congregations might consider discarding this requirement, or else allowing for temporary commitment to it. Neither celibacy nor permanent commitment is necessary under the association model, and their elimination would remove a major obstacle to membership growth. But it is not enough merely to remove obstacles; associational religious congregations must develop and advertise positive incentives to encourage new members to join. Opus Dei has grown to be three times as large as the largest mainstream religious order, at least in part because its members perceive it as offering educational benefits and access to ecclesiastical and civil power.[58] Associational religious congregations, in their turn, may choose to emphasize and advertise the opportunities they offer for participation in a particular ministry or mission, their opportunities for mentoring and weak tie networking, or simply their friendship bonds with each other. All of these are positive attractions, but perhaps not unique to religious life. Prospective recruits might still ask why they couldn't partake of the ministry, and enjoy the friendship ties and networking, without membership in the religious congregation. The challenge for associational congregations will be to convince young Catholics that religious life offers a unique and valuable way to experience these benefits.

In conclusion, one might say that the associational and the communitarian models for religious life are, to some extent, mirror images of each other in the strengths and weaknesses they have for successful recruitment. The intentional community possesses a distinctive form of commitment which may be perceived as more appropriate to the call of Christ, but the necessary mechanisms currently available to foster and maintain this commitment are perceived as psychologically unhealthy and as antithetical to some basic American values. Unless they can develop effective commitment mechanisms which are more congruent with American culture, communitarian religious congregations will have to await the appearance of charismatic founders or refounders before they can expect to attract new members. The association, by contrast, is an accepted and valued mode of interaction in our society; observers from De Toqueville's time to the present day have remarked upon our tendency to form and join them. But religious congregations have yet to articulate a distinctive identity under the associational model. Until they do so, it is unlikely that they will become exceptions to the dismal mortality statistics on former intentional communities that attempt to become associations.

The Role of the Bureaucratic Model

Religious congregations are perhaps least compatible with the bureaucratic model, and so it is probably neither appropriate nor enlightening to outline a separate set of recruitment strategies appropriate to this group type. Bureaucratic values, however, do exert some influence upon the current vocation practices of religious congregations. Since bureaucratic standards are not compatible with the intentional community model at all, and only partially congruent with the associational model, it can be expected that their contribution to the vocation strategies of the latter two models will be confusing at best, and disruptive and negative at worst. The following section will list and discuss a few of the areas in which bureaucratic procedures and values affect the vocation efforts of religious congregations.

BUREAUCRATIZATION AND RELIGIOUS RECRUITMENT

Segmentation of Roles

A key feature of a bureaucratic organization is the division of its work into specialized positions, each with its own job description, and the tendency which this division engenders for each worker to be concerned only with his or her assigned tasks. In bureaucratized religious congregations, the establishment of a vocation office or committee may be perceived as absolving the rest of the membership from recruitment activities, even if the office disseminates a stream of material saying otherwise. The vocation director or the members of the vocation committee become "the experts," and other members may be tempted to shift to them the responsibility for contacting any individuals who express interest in joining, and for explaining the program to them. And since the vocation staff cannot shoulder the entire burden of all this personal contact, they may tend to substitute the publication of vocation brochures, or the mailing of vocation week directives to the other members—most of whom will ignore them. Researchers are divided on how successful a vocation office is.[59] Most probably such an office is quite valuable for the complementary function of coordinating and systematizing the vocation program in the congregation at large. *But it can never substitute for the indispensable recruitment requirement of both intentional communities and associations: the personal involvement of each member in actively seeking out and encouraging potential recruits to enter, even before these individuals express an interest in doing so.* Vocation directors may object that they never intended to substitute for individual effort, and, in fact, they may insist that a large part of their work involves trying to persuade the rest of the congregation to accept their rightful responsibility for membership recruitment. But the bureaucratic standards implicit in the very establishment of a separate vocation office will undermine their efforts to involve the rest of the congregation, even as it provides the essential overall coordination that bureaucratic procedures do so well.

Credentialism

Ideally, in a bureaucracy, hiring is done according to universally applied standards. Job applicants are expected to possess a particular set of credentials in order to be considered for a job: an MBA degree, for example, or the ability to program a computer. There may be the tendency in a religious congregation to set up similar preliminary standards for potential entrants. Interested recruits may be told to obtain a college degree or work experience before applying, and may be subtly discouraged if their high school background is not adequate for higher education or a steady job. Orders with seminaries may be especially likely to do this kind of screening.

Admittedly, the establishment of these standards may have been done for very valid reasons. Communities may have wished to avoid the "class system" which used to exist in some orders, whereby the less-educated members were relegated to inferior tasks and denied, formally or informally, access to power in the congregation. Society at large also sets bureaucratic standards for hospital administrators, nurses, teachers, and the like. The days are past when a congregation could simply assign an uneducated but talented member to a position of ministerial responsibility and have him/her learn on the job. And, in the present days of fiscal strain, most communities are simply unable to finance the college education of new members.

But limiting recruitment to those who possess the right credentials shuts out the very part of the Catholic population which is likely to be most receptive to joining the congregation. The communitarian religious congregations of the past drew members at least partly because entering religious life was a "step up" for a second-generation immigrant, and provided an education and a professional career which could not otherwise be obtained. Associations, too, must offer some concrete incentives for persons to join them. The fastest-growing association in Catholicism today provides attractive scholarships which enable talented but poor young people to rise to positions of power and influence.[60]

Middle-class, assimilated American Catholics simply have too many other career options for religious life—whether communitarian or associational—to compete successfully. The most likely recruits to religious congregations are the less-advantaged segments of the Catholic population—notably Latinos, who will comprise the majority of U.S. Catholics in less than twenty years. It has been estimated that there should be five times as many Latinos preparing for religious life as there are now, but they have been screened out, or put off from even considering a religious vocation, by their lack of the proper educational credentials.[61] It is no accident that the parts of the world still gaining vocations are Asia and Africa, where religious life provides education and status to young people, especially women, who could not otherwise attain it, and in parts of eastern Europe, where it is an expression of nationalism:

> Aside from Poland and Yugoslavia—the only exceptions in the West to the drying up of religious vocations—the sole continents where the ideals of St. Ignatius continue to attract young men are Asia and, especially in the most recent years, Africa . . . it is predicted that, if present trends continue, within 15 years the country with the most Jesuits will be India.[62]

If religious congregations make active attempts to attract "less qualified" recruits, they will have to be careful to allow these new members full power and equal status within the community. A recent study of the growth of Protestant churches in nineteenth century America pointed out that it was precisely those churches which were not dominated by an upper-class elite, and which offered a voice to the less-educated masses, that experienced explosive growth.[63] Similarly, Catholicism is rapidly losing its Latino members to fundamentalist sects, which provide them with opportunities to control their own denominational organization which are unavailable in the Catholic Church.

> The Protestant and Pentecostal churches are making great inroads into the Hispanic community. They are perceived as churches of the poor and for the poor (whether this be the reality or not). . . . They are basically lay churches in which anyone willing to spend time in training can become an apostle.[64]

Religious life cannot hope to attract new members, of whatever ethnicity, if it does not offer them true equality and the opportunity for full participation, as well as, for working-class recruits, the opportunity to develop their skills and talents.

The admission of working class or minority recruits, however, will raise a second problem: whether an increased number of members from a different culture might exacerbate the heterogeneity—already strained by cross-generational differences—of communitarian congregations. A potential for serious division exists here, which may only be able to be solved by establishing financially and governmentally independent provinces for the different groups. Associational congregations will have fewer problems in this respect, since they are more loosely organized internally. But they must still guard against any tendency to shut minority members out of the core group that makes the order's policy decisions.

Universality and Impartiality

Finally, bureaucratic organizations attempt to standardize procedures, so that they can be fairly and impartially applied. While this is a welcome antidote to the abuses of authority that often occurred in intentional communities,[65] it can sometimes be counter-productive. Potential recruits, especially recruits to communitarian congregations, may be disconcerted to be told that a general policy cannot be bent if they are from a slightly different background than the average for which the policy was written. Some applicants may be older, for example, and yet be expected to wait and gain further work experience. Or a transfer from another community may be asked to go through the novitiate again. The inflexible application of such rules will seem at variance with the "family spirit" which may have attracted the recruit to the community.

Summary

Bureaucratic standards, while efficient and perhaps unavoidable, can counteract the requirements which a religious congregation—whether associational or communitarian—must follow in order to attract new members. The establishment of a separate vocation office may relieve the rest of the congregation from exerting themselves to approach potential recruits, even if those employed in that office are actively trying to involve them. The requirement of a set level of credentials may discourage the very groups which would be most interested in joining. And universalistic standards of treatment may not be applicable to recruits from non-standard backgrounds. The challenge for religious congregations is to be aware of the benefits and the liabilities of bureaucratic procedures, and to use them only insofar as they are beneficial.

Conclusions

This chapter has set up an extremely difficult agenda for religious communities. Not only must they decide which of the potentially contradictory requirements for associational and communitarian recruitment best apply to their particular situation, they must also enunciate, for the first time, how these standards

fit in with contemporary American culture. And they must carefully balance out whether and how to apply bureaucratic standards
to the procedures they choose. With such a daunting agenda, it
may not seem fair to end the chapter without supplying some road
map to follow. But the construction of such guidelines is beyond
the ability of any one writer. A concerted effort of many writers,
researchers and congregations is needed—and is already taking
place, to some extent. Religious congregations must first be aware
of the requirements outlined in this chapter for making their
particular order attractive to potential members. They must next
actively experiment with devising ways to fulfill these requirements—and involve as many members as possible in doing so.
Already-established groups such as the National Sisters Vocation
Conference or the Bishops' Project 13 for Hispanic vocations
must offer as many opportunities as possible for communities to
get together and share which strategies work and which do not.
Some suggestions have been given in this chapter for activities
such as role playing the invitation of a potential member to "come
and see"; these suggestions should be tried, evaluated, and re-
fined. More need to be developed and shared.

Even with all these efforts, it is possible that many religious
congregations will not be able to attract sufficient new recruits to
survive. The communitarian congregations that continue into the
growth and expansion phase of the sixth cycle of religious life will
be those that meet the requirements for communitarian recruitment—those whose members are joyful and enthusiastic about the
life they live, and who can foster this joy and enthusiasm by a set
of commitment mechanisms that are psychologically healthy and
not antithetical to contemporary culture. The successful associational congregations will be those which can evidence the concrete benefits to be gained by membership. My personal candidate
for such a benefit—for women religious at least—would be the
weak ties, mentoring opportunities and friendship networks
which religious life offers. This is a tremendously empowering
resource, and one which is otherwise unavailable to many women
in our society. But associational congregations will have to de-

velop a more effective way to make Catholic lay women aware that they possess such a network. Finally, all successful religious congregations—communitarian and associational—will be the ones whose members are actively involved in inviting new young people to join them.

Paradoxically, the way to growth may not be for religious to concentrate self-consciously on the ways their congregation falls short of the goal of successful membership attraction. A better strategy might be for those in a religious congregation, once they are aware of the areas that must be changed, to consider them as a by-product of a greater goal: that of witnessing to the benefits—spiritual, emotional and utilitarian—of religious life. Chapter 7 will outline one possible way this might be done. First, however, we will consider another question: the role of ministerial institutions in associational and communitarian religious life.

6

Institutionalized Ministries
and Religious Life

The existence of their present ministerial institutions, and the prospect of institutionalizing new works or projects, confront religious congregations with several potentially problematic choices. On the one hand, institutions in our culture are almost always bureaucratic ones, and bureaucracies have a way of perpetuating their existence and of organizing their operations independently of the changing needs of their surrounding environment. On the other hand, failure to institutionalize may tie a ministerial work too closely to the personal commitment of a small group of individuals—or perhaps to only one person. The longevity of the work may come to depend upon the ability of a single individual (increasingly, in most religious communities, a single *elderly* individual) to devote his/her time to nurture it. When that religious decides (or is forced by age or illness) to retire from the work, it may dissolve, whether or not the need for it still exists. Failure to institutionalize a ministry can also deprive it of the power or influence necessary to succeed in an environment which is increasingly dominated by other large-scale institutions.

Preliminary Definitions

In this chapter, the term "institution" will be used in a colloquial rather than in a strictly sociological sense, and will refer to a specific organization such as a hospital, college, or social work agency.[1] Defined in this manner, institutions are characterized by their stable continuance over time (despite sometimes complete turnovers in administration, staff and clientele), by their possession of fixed assets (buildings, land, pension funds, etc.), and by their occupation of a specific field of action (the psychiatric care of AIDS patients, for example, or remedial college preparation for ghetto youth) which is recognized and accepted by the other institutions in their environment. In the United States and in most other societies, institutions are also legally incorporated by the state.

"Institutionalization," therefore, can be defined as the process by which a ministerial work, originally founded by and dependent upon the initiative of a single person or a small group of people, grows in size and develops the characteristics listed in the preceding paragraph. Institutionalization often occurs gradually over a period of years. But it is also possible for a work to be institutionalized immediately upon its inception. This was often the case prior to Vatican II, when a congregation would buy or build a building, open a new school or hospital in it, and staff it with workers, all in the space of a year or two.

Choices in Ministerial Institutionalization

CHOICE I: BUREAUCRATIC VS. NON-BUREAUCRATIC INSTITUTIONALIZATION

The Process of Bureaucratization

Institutions do not have to be bureaucratic. It is possible for an institution to continue over time and to possess fixed assets without the hierarchical division of labor, extensive written rules and files, or universalistic hiring and promotion procedures that characterize bureaucracies. Indeed, the early institutions of most religious orders—their schools, hospitals, orphanages and the like—often had very few bureaucratic qualities. They were staffed almost entirely by members of the congregation, many of whom were assigned to positions of authority and responsibility without possessing the formal credentials that bureaucracies require. Religious were expected to be generalists, performing whatever tasks needed to be done—there were few job descriptions outlining a formalized division of labor. Since the workers had all been socialized into the common ideology and value system of the religious community, there was less need for a large number of written rules in their institutions. Comparatively unbureaucratized, therefore, the early ministerial institutions of a congregation functioned quite well for many years and built impressive physical plants to house their operations.

As was pointed out in chapter 3, however, many aspects of modern society push the ministerial institutions of religious congregations toward conformity with the bureaucratic model. Clients, employees (both religious and lay), suppliers, banks, and government agencies expect other institutions to follow standard bureaucratic procedures, and have the power to penalize them if they do not. Clients may go elsewhere, employees may strike, banks refuse loans, and government agencies decertify the ministerial institution which does not have a credentialed staff, written policies and procedures, and other bureaucratic trappings. The increased size of an institution usually requires at least some bureaucratization in order to run efficiently. Isomorphism with the surrounding organizational environment also encourages an institution to bureaucratize.[2] It would be hard, for example, for a hospital to reorganize itself along non-bureaucratic lines and to eliminate the division of labor between emergency room nurses and resident doctors (even though the former are usually more experienced than the latter), or to mentor capable and ambitious workers from orderly to LPN to RN to MD to hospital administrator. Professional associations are not set up to include doctor-nurses or nurse-orderlies—indeed, a major purpose of these associations is precisely to prevent such hybrids from encroaching upon the exclusive preserve of the full professionals. Training schools provide workers only within defined disciplines; government accrediting agencies also mandate the divisions. Even the restructuring of a hospital floor from functional patient care to total patient care (which involves a moderate amount of debureaucratization) is often difficult. Finally, the bureaucratic model has become standard in our culture to such an extent that the administrators and workers in a given ministerial institution may find it impossible even to envision a non-bureaucratic alternative.

Implications

If a ministerial institution bureaucratizes, the question may arise whether it can claim really to be different from secular institutions in the same field. Is it really evident to the patient in the hospital bed or the nurse on the floor that he/she is in a Catholic institution founded upon the mission statement of a particular congregation? Isomorphism with other, bureaucratized hospitals may have taken place to such an extent that the philosophy which supposedly underlies the very existence of the congregation's ministry has been reduced to generalized phrases, largely decoupled from the day-to-day operations of the institution. An institution may even find itself behaving in ways which run counter to the congregation's ideology (but which conform to the bureaucratic ideal)—treating employees impersonally, for example, or turning away indigent clients, or buying supplies from the cheapest source rather than from a minority business. Another implication of bureaucratization concerns the hiring and promotion of workers. To the extent that the bureaucratic standards of universality and credentialism are applied, a congregational institution may find itself hiring "better qualified" lay applicants instead of its own members, and even promoting them to top policy-making positions.

> A problem lurking down deep in the debate . . . is the "instrumental" character of the religious man's or woman's commitment to one or the other professional track [which] we see . . . as a way of fulfilling our religious vocation. That

has become increasingly difficult as we work in hospitals or schools which are no longer manageable as extensions of our religious community. Size, sophistication and government funding have made them new entities. We compete for jobs, we are promoted, we are fired. It is a very new religious vocation. The institutionalization of the church in the United States grew in response to perceived needs of the nineteenth and early twentieth centuries. To what need does my new vocation respond?[3]

The institution may thus gradually lose the "flavor" or spirit that had marked it as a work of this particular religious congregation. Also, as was mentioned in chapter 3, critics of bureaucratic credentialism claim that such standards serve more to discriminate against women and other minority workers than to choose the most capable applicant. The vaunted "rational impartiality" of the ideal bureaucracy in fact disguises a pervasive race- and gender-based stratification system:

> "Rationality" requires as a condition of its existence the simultaneous creation of the realm of the personal, the emotional, the sexual, the "irrational." Bureaucracy creates the illusion of ordered rationality but could not exist unless the other side were there too. Masculine rationality is constructed in opposition to the feminine, as a denial of the feminine, but does not exist without it. Rather than existing in separate social spaces, public and private occur simultaneously within one social space.[4]

For these reasons, feminist organizational theorists have called for the adoption of more empowering, non-bureaucratic practices in business, government and social welfare organizations. In such a climate, the further bureaucratization of ministeries run by religious communities—especially communities of women religious —may be going counter to their best interests. Women religious may find not only that they have lost control of the day-to-day direction of their ministerial institutions, but also that the paths of upward career mobility in these institutions, formerly open to them, are now blocked.

But if the bureaucratization of an order's institutions is accompanied by negative as well as positive outcomes, failure to bureaucratize also has implications. To begin with, it ought to be noted that all ministerial institutions have been bureaucratized to some extent. The pressures outlined in the preceding section are too strong. Some congregations, however, especially those which have retained more of their communitarian characteristics, have also retained many non-bureaucratic elements in their institutions. Schools and colleges may still hire and promote community members over more objectively qualified outsiders, there may be unwritten rules and informal communication networks to which lay employees have less access, religious workers may do extra tasks not in their job descriptions and be more personally involved in the institution than would be usual in a purely bureaucratic one.

There are advantages to non-bureaucratic organization. Morale and commitment may be higher, especially among the religious who work in the institution, than would be the case in a more formal and impersonal bureaucracy. This enthusiasm and dedication may mean that the organization can do more with less money, for the workers will devote extra hours of work without pay. Non-bureaucratic institutions may also have more flexibility to innovate, without having to go through several layers of bureaucratic hierarchy to do so. And, as was mentioned above, non-bureaucratic ministries may offer those women religious who are less credentialed an avenue for career advancement that bureaucratized ones do not.

However, disadvantages also accompany the failure to bureaucratize, especially when the majority of an institution's employees no longer belong to the sponsoring congregation. The "inside track" and informal communication network possessed by the religious employees may be perceived as clique-like and exclusive by the lay workers. The lack of formal rules, too, poses problems for religious institutions, comparable to those noted by Perrow for businesses:

> Many managers feel that "freedom" lies in the sort of situation where their supervisor says to them: "There are not many regulations in this place. You will understand the job in a month or two, and you make your own decisions. No red tape—you are expected to take command; make the decisions off your own bat as they arise. I am against a lot of rules or regulations, and we do not commit too much to paper." In my experience, a manager in such a situation has virtually no "freedom to act" at all. He starts making decisions and his boss sends for him to say: "Look here, Jones, I am sorry to tell you that you have made two rather serious mistakes in the course of reorganizing your work. You have promoted one man to supervisor who is not the next man due for promotion in the factory, and you have engaged five additional machinists, a decision you should have referred to me because we have some surplus men in this category in an adjacent factory." Now Jones might well say: "You said there were no regulations but, in fact, you have already mentioned the existence of two: one concerned with promotion and the other with increase of establishment. Please detail these regulations to me precisely, so that I can work to them in the future, and let me know now of any further regulations which bear upon my work."
>
> In practice, Jones probably says nothing of the kind, because he does not think in this way; to him regulations are stumbling blocks in the path of those wishing to display initiative. He will proceed, over the years, to learn, by making mistakes, of the whole array of regulations which . . . do in fact exist.[5]

There is also no assurance that non-bureaucratic institutions will be more flexible than bureaucratic ones. They may be, but there are also many ministerial organizations, however non-bureaucratic, where "We've always done it this way" puts a stop to any innovation. Thus, it is quite possible that the procedures of a less bureaucratized institution will be profoundly alienating, especially to those workers who are not members of the congregational in-group. Given that the universal, "scientific" standards of modern bureaucracies are a primary value in our culture, disaffected workers in less-bureaucratized institutions will have a well-developed vocabulary and ideology readily available to articulate their complaints.

CHOICE II: PERSISTENCE VS. INSTITUTIONAL DEMISE

Another aspect of institutions is their tendency to persist unchanged, or to grow and develop along lines pre-determined by their internal dynamics rather than by the needs of their surrounding environment. This poses a problem when the environment changes. Environmental imperatives may make it desirable for an institution to alter its operations radically, and may even eliminate altogether the very reason for the institution's existence. *But neither fundamental reorganization nor voluntary demise is likely in an established institution.* For example, the original reason for Catholic hospitals was to provide needed health care for the poor. Today, Medicaid regulations, soaring health care costs, staff shortages, Diagnostic Related Groups, overbedding and a host of other considerations have drastically affected the way these hospitals do business. Some cannot make ends meet and are in danger of closing—whether or not this would be a desirable outcome for their (usually impoverished) clientele. Others find themselves in a competitive market with other half-empty hospitals, providing identical services to a smaller number of middle-class patients while other health needs in the area go unmet. But it is rare to see a hospital voluntarily dissolving or radically reorienting its mandate in order to serve, for example, only homeless AIDS patients. Similarly, the original reason for the parochial school system was to educate immigrant Catholic youth, and to enable their assimilation to American culture without the loss of their Catholicism in the process. Today, most non-Latino Catholics inhabit middle-class suburbs, where the public school system is often more attractive than the local parish school (if, indeed, the latter even exists). Many middle-class Catholic suburbanites are thoroughly assimilated "cultural Catholics" whose beliefs have moved closer to those of the Protestant mainstream, and who may see little value in a separate educational system. They have also had far fewer children than their parents; the "Baby Bust" generation fills only a fraction of the classrooms that were needed for the Baby Boomers. Meanwhile, many of the new migrants filling our cities are not Catholic, and Latinos are increasingly converting to Protestant churches. Yet a given parochial school, whether in the inner city or in the suburbs, may not be adapting to this changed environment, or may be doing so only slowly.

"Permanently Failing Organizations"

Institutions which fail to adapt successfully to their changed environment may nevertheless remain for years, operating at half capacity, chronically in the red financially, or simply failing to produce the results which are the stated purpose for their existence. A recent analysis terms such institutions "permanently failing organizations": those that persist even though they are performing poorly and not meeting the expectations of their owners or sponsors.[6] Why does such a seemingly counter-intuitive situation occur?

> Most people are more concerned with maintaining existing organizations than with maximizing organizational performance. As long as performance is high, the interests of those wishing to maintain an organization—often those dependent on it, such as the workers or buyers of its product—correspond with those wishing to meet official objectives (e.g. profit)—often those who control it, such as owners or managers. . . . However, should exogenous events cause performance to deteriorate, *which occurs sooner or later in almost all*

organizations, then the interests of those seeking to maintain organizations and of those seeking high performance become antagonistic, sometimes dramatically so. Those seeking performance—owners invested with property rights or officials having legal authority—attempt to change organizations. . . . But those wishing to maintain existing organizational arrangements, numerically the majority but not always powerful, oppose change. Change is opposed because of the benefits for the majority, such as good salaries or promotion opportunities. *Thus organizations are maintained for reasons of self-interest.*[7] [italics mine]

One of the book's four case studies applies the concept of permanent failure to the sort of congregationally-supported institutions we are discussing in this chapter.[8] Cathedral High School in Los Angeles, owned by the archdiocese, had been operated since 1924 by the Christian Brothers to educate working class, immigrant boys. By the 1980s its formerly Italian student body had become largely Latino, ninety percent of whom continued on to college and became the leaders of Los Angeles' Hispanic community. As far as the Christian Brothers, the students, and their parents were concerned, Cathedral High School was a success. It was operating at full capacity and fulfilling a valued educational function.

The archdiocese of Los Angeles, however, saw matters slightly differently. Three other Catholic boys' high schools existed in central Los Angeles, and all three were suffering declining enrollment. Some sort of consolidation seemed to be a more desirable and efficient use of archdiocesan resources. Cathedral High School's physical plant was the oldest of the four and needed the most costly repairs. And unlike the other three schools, it was also sitting on prime urban land, for which a buyer could readily be found. In July 1984, therefore, the archdiocese announced that it had contracted to sell Cathedral High School to a Hong Kong developer.

"The decision to close Cathedral High School was consistent with the businesslike approach to most matters taken by the

Los Angeles Archdiocese. Monsignor Benjamin Hawkes, vicar general of the archdiocese, had built the archdiocese into the second wealthiest in the United States through several decades of development, building and real estate transactions."[9] But although the decision to close Cathedral may have been efficient and businesslike, several key groups had a vested interest in the school's continuation. The Christian Brothers and the lay staff had not been consulted or even informed of the decision ahead of time. The students and their parents worried that they would lose a key educational resource for upward mobility. Alumni had sentimental attachments to their alma mater. The Latino community, many of whose leaders had graduated from Cathedral, saw it as a slap in the face. These groups mobilized in a "Save Cathedral High School" campaign.

> The Christian Brothers, who stood to gain nothing from the sale, publicly accused the archdiocese's lobbyists of lying to the Los Angeles City Council and privately threatened to sue the archdiocese for defamation. Various politicians seized upon the threatened closing of Cathedral High School as a Hispanic cause; ultimately, Mayor Tom Bradley sided with supporters of the school and presented Cathedral with a $100,000 check from an "anonymous donor," to be used to rehabilitate the campus.[10]

In December 1985 the archdiocese bowed to the pressure and backed down. All four high schools were to remain open. In the aftermath, archdiocesan officials have been reluctant to consolidate *any* of the schools, even though the other three high schools are each operating at under fifty percent of capacity and even Cathedral High School can now boast only eight-five percent. Despite more than one thousand empty seats, officials stated "that the archdiocese will not initiate discussion of closing any schools, and that any proposals for mergers or consolidations will have to come from the schools themselves. Underenrolled schools, therefore, have become a fact of life for the Los Angeles Archdiocese, though we suspect that the final chapter in consolidation has not yet been written."[11] At least three of the four schools have become permanently failing organizations.

Conflicting Interests and Permanent Failure

Ministerial institutions become "permanently failing" if, once conflict develops between those who desire to adapt to a changing environment through organizational change or dissolution and those who have a vested interest in the status quo, the latter group has more power. One type of conflict, such as the one described in the preceding section, may be between the owners (the archdiocese, a religious congregation), who are interested in the efficient use of resources, and "dependent actors," who are less concerned than the owners about the official objectives of the institution "but are, at the same time, dependent on the organization for other benefits, including wages (for workers), goods and services (for customers), and the organization's contribution to the local economy (for political leaders)."[12] In the case of Cathedral High School, the power of the dependent actors—the Christian Brothers, the Latino community, the students, parents and alumni—was greater than that of the owner—the archdiocese. The schools remained open even though, according to financial and enrollment standards, at least three of them were "failing." This sort of conflict—between the clerical hierarchy who control needed funds and the Catholic laity who use the schools—is evidently a common one. A 1976 study found that, among the laity, there was ". . . a vigorous endorsement of the parochial school system, *and more financial resources available than the church has yet been willing to use.*"[13] [italics mine] More recent studies have confirmed this finding that the clergy are less supportive of parochial schools than the laity.[14]

Another sort of conflict might develop in institutions which have become "family firms." The *Los Angeles Examiner* was the only newspaper personally started by William Randolph Hearst, and his descendants still retain a sentimental attachment to it. They are unwilling to sell it or to modify its editorial policy, even though it has suffered a seventy-five percent decline in readership over the past two decades.[15] Similarly, members of a religious congregation may have an emotional tie to a given ministerial institution: "We can't close *that* school—that was the first school started by our Mother Foundress," or "—that was the first site of our Motherhouse," or "—half of our sisters graduated from there." In this situation it is the owners who wish the institution to remain open, and who resist environmental pressures to close it.

There is a third possible source of conflict leading to permanent organizational failure. This would be when some powerful outside agency, while not dependent on the institution in any strict sense, nevertheless has other reasons for opposing the organization's change or dissolution. For example, the bishop of Diocese X may have his eye on an appointment to Rome (or on a more prestigious archdiocese, or on a cardinal's hat), and may not wish his ambitions derailed by negative publicity about his diocese. Hospital Y in the main city of Diocese X serves the inner-city poor, is strapped for funds, and is in danger of closing. The area is overbedded with private hospitals, which, however, are reluctant to accept Hospital Y's impoverished clientele. Closing Hospital Y would result in a political struggle and much publicity. In such a situation, Hospital Y may experience strong pressure from both the diocese and the private hospitals to remain open, even if neither of these pressure groups is willing to contribute the funds which Hospital Y desperately needs.

Summary

All organizations tend, over time, toward permanent failure because they involve so many varied interests and dependent actors who resist even necessary change. The institutions which religious congregations are likely to sponsor are even more likely than most organizations to develop these problems. Since a ministerial institution often has goals other than simple efficiency or financial profit, and since these goals are less readily measured, it becomes harder for the congregational owners to prove that they are not being met, and easier for the dependent actors to argue that the work should remain in operation. Unmeasurable goals are also less clearly defined, and different actors may have differing ideas of what they are. In times of dispute over organizational change, hitherto unsuspected differences of interpretation may surface and cause even more dissension:

> The theory of permanent failure anticipates why change occurs slowly and with difficulty in these settings. Given diversity on ends or as means to ends those wishing change —even when they have formal authority—will often be confronted by others whose interests are served best by non-change. To the extent that the latter are able to mobilize effectively, stalemate results. The theory also anticipates why many positions, leadership roles in particular, prove so frustrating in these settings.[16]

Religious congregations, therefore, may find themselves tied down to permanently failing institutions, which sap congregational resources without ever quite delivering on their promised goals, and which monopolize energies better expended elsewhere.

CHOICE III: INSTITUTIONALIZATION VS. REFUSAL TO INSTITUTIONALIZE

If the organizational dynamics described in the preceding section so often result in permanent failure, perhaps it would be better to avoid institutionalizing a ministry in the first place. Religious in some congregations have questioned whether human and financial resources should be committed to institution-building at this stage in their existence, the more so if such institutions are likely to persist beyond their usefulness and become a liability in the future.

There are, however, also liabilities to *not* institutionalizing a ministry. Failure to institutionalize a work—to buy or build a physical plant and to commit sufficient personnel to run it—will impact negatively on the stability of the congregation's commitment to that work. While this certainly eliminates the danger of becoming tied to a permanently failing organization, it also means that some worthwhile works may be abandoned prematurely, simply because the lease has expired on the building, or the one religious whose personal commitment was the lifeblood of the ministry has had a heart attack. Certain ministries may require incorporation with the state (often the first step to institutionalization), or a large bank loan, or simply several decades' worth of operation in order to carve out a recognized field of action vis-à-vis other institutional actors. Reluctance to institutionalize may mean that these sorts of ministries will not be undertaken.

Institutionalization—both the bureaucratized and the non-bureaucratized variety—is also a source of power, which individual actors simply do not have:

> Natural persons [are] relatively powerless in their relationship with organizations. Customers lack information about product quality and safety, but corporations use market research to learn about customer preference and spending patterns. Students know very little about the quality of education available at different schools to which they apply, but colleges require prospective students to provide considerable personal and academic information. Workers have few alternatives when faced with a corporation that decides to shut down and move production to a lower wage area.[17]

In the past, their institutional strength had enabled religious congregations to hold their own when necessary against other organized elements in the church, to a far greater extent than would have been possible for them as individuals. Ewens documents this for women religious in the nineteenth century United States:

> Bishops and priests came to have a healthy respect for the power of sisters, and with good reason. The sisters were important influences in the community, and ran most of the

Church's charitable institutions. In disagreements, sisters fought for their rights and usually won. Then, too, they could and did vote with their feet, or threatened to, when the occasion warranted it.[18]

In the network of institutions that makes up modern western society, the power of one organization over another in a given situation depends on the former's provision of valued resources which the latter needs, or its ability to ensure the recognition of its authority in a particular domain.[19] To the extent that religious congregations were the recognized providers, through their institutionalized ministries, of services which the church had defined as essential to its mission in the United States, they had a certain amount of power vis-à-vis the diocesan hierarchy. For women religious, especially, this experience of organizational power was and is a valuable resource. Attempts by contemporary women's groups to establish women's banks, women-owned recording companies, and women-run publishing houses are examples of how the power of an established institution is necessary when confronting an environment composed of similar organizations. Without their institutional base, religious congregations, male and female, would have a much weaker voice in their dealings with the institutional church.

Religious congregations, through their ministerial institutions, may also have a degree of power within the larger community, which can be wielded to promote systemic change. One example of this is the attempts by many religious groups to use their investments or their pension funds to encourage corporate responsibility. Large scale ministerial institutions may also possess the power to alter neighborhood land use, influence local or state legislators, or reduce the unemployment rate of local populations. To the extent that values other than bureaucratic efficiency still animate religious institutions, they may be able to use their power in ways that are unusual, and to promote the values of the gospel as no individual could. On the other hand, strong pressures will exist for them to operate in a manner isomorphic with the other bureaucratic institutions in the area. If this happens, outsiders affected by the religious institution's policies may not be able to detect any differences between its actions and those of its secular counterparts.

Summary

None of these choices—bureaucratization or non-bureaucratization, continuance or dissolution, institutionalization or refusal to institutionalize—are easy to make. All, in fact, involve vested interests on both sides (and numerous permutations of middle-ground opinions as well), which make it difficult, if not impossible, to explore the ramifications of all the options. The process of choosing is usually intensely politicized, and is in itself disruptive of organizational functioning. Even if the emotional involvement of the parties involved could be suspended in a particular case, formidable obstacles would still remain. Studies of organizational decision-making have emphasized that institutional actors are only *intendedly* rational: they would *like* to make the best decision in a given instance, but they never possess all the information they would need to determine what it is.[20] And the "search costs"—time, organizational resources, money—attached to exploring alternatives may be too great for decision makers to indulge in such activity for very long.

As a result, many institutions simply "drift into" making a particular choice. They bureaucratize because similar organizations have done so, or they fail to bureaucratize a key aspect of their functioning because too many people prefer things as they are.[21] They continue in operation even though they are losing money (or students, or staff), until a reorganization or dissolution is forced upon them. In previous decades, the desirability of institutionalizing a ministerial work was taken for granted; now many congregations allow one of their members to begin a new work on their own incentive, but never seriously consider the possibility of institutionalizing it beyond that individual member's personal commitment. Disruptive conflict and debate may be avoided by such unexamined drifting, but at the price of possible outcomes that may not be the best, either for the ministry or for the congregation itself. Eventually, a choice will always be made —an institution is created or it is not, it bureaucratizes or it doesn't, it continues or is dissolved. In spite of the difficulties involved with specifically examining such issues, therefore, it would be well if congregational decision-makers could undertake such examinations, and could utilize the theories and findings of sociological research in their deliberations.

A Note on Institutionalized Ministries in Associational Religious Life

Most of the material in this chapter thus far applies primarily to communitarian religious organizations. By their very nature, associational orders will have less difficulty with some of the choices than communitarian ones will. The associational model, for example, is more compatible with bureaucratic procedures, and thus the application of impartial hiring and promotion standards, or the decoupling of the association's ideology from the day-to-day running of the institution, will prove less problematic than such issues had been for intentional communities. The choice of whether to bureaucratize or not is thus fairly easy for an association, and the decision is usually on the more culturally-congruent side of bureaucratization.

The second of the three choices—whether to institutionalize in the first place—is also less difficult for associational congregations to make, but this one has more potentially serious ramifications. *It is unlikely that an association can commit itself to supporting institutions in any concrete way other than financially.* Associations do sponsor institutions (for example, the Shriners, a fraternal association, sponsor several hospitals for burned children), but their members rarely work there except, perhaps, on a voluntary basis.

This fact has several implications for a religious congregation that has moved toward the associational model. Many institutionalized ministries inherited from its communitarian past may officially belong to such a congregation, but the order will no longer be able to request or require its members to work there. When one considers the order's declining numbers and aging membership, it will become less and less likely that *any* of the congregation's religious will work in these institutions. The institution will also probably have separate sources of funds (tuition fees, for example, or Blue Cross and Medicare payments), and so be relatively independent of the congregation financially. The order's sponsorship will then be reduced to the occupation of a certain percentage of the seats on the institution's board of directors. This distancing from the day-to-day operation of the institution will have several results. It will probably be inevitable that further decoupling will occur between the philosophy articulated by the board and the day-to-day running of the institution, in which few if any religious are now involved. (In fact, since the members of an associational congregation may not themselves agree on a communal ideology, other than in the most general terms, there may *be* no distinctive philosophy to impose on its institutions.) A divergence of interests may also arise between the managers and staff employed to operate and work in the institution and the religious congregation which retains sponsorship. In some cases, this may lead to the congregation becoming trapped in a permanently failing organization, which continues to occupy the community's energies and perhaps even a limited amount of its financial resources and membership, because the dependent actors who actually run the institution now possess more power than its nominal sponsors. In other cases, the congregation may end up severing all connection with the institution, thus losing an avenue of service in that ministry.

A second implication of the associational model for the sponsorship of ministerial institutions involves the movement of the order into new works. Associational congregations will be much less likely to found new institutions when their members move into a new area of service.[22] As a result, new ministries are likely to be dependent on the dedication and physical health of one or a few religious. Many individual religious may also be reluctant to initiate new ministries, especially if they are in remote or distant areas, because they will have to "go it alone." In pre-Vatican II days, a congregation that decided to open a school on an Indian reservation, establish a clinic for migrant workers, or set up a settlement house in the inner city would have been able to assign five or six religious to the task. But since associational congregations do not *assign* members to ministries, it would be the individual member's task to locate by himself/herself sufficient fellow workers to begin an apostolate. This may be very difficult to do. The alternative, of course, is for the religious to work for some already-established institution involved in the same work. But such an institution may not exist, especially if the need is a new one. And working for another institution may deprive the religious—especially a woman religious—of the opportunity for upward mobility into policy-making positions.

Conclusion

The question of whether or not to institutionalize a new ministry, or of what to do with already-institutionalized ministries, will most likely continue to occupy congregations in the years ahead. Of course, should the congregation itself dissolve, or even move to a purely associational model, most of the questions raised in this chapter will become moot. It is essential, however, for those congregations who wish to survive, either as intentional communities or as some associational-communitarian combination, to address the issue of ministerial institutions. Merely allowing the issue to drift toward its own resolution will not assure an optimal outcome, either for the congregation or for the people —staff, administration and clients—who depend on its institutions. Training congregational decision-makers in business management, however, is also not enough for addressing these choices adequately. Business management books and courses tend to take for granted only one side of each question—they assume the desirability of bureaucratization over non-bureaucratization, of organizational continuance over dissolution, and of institutionalization over failure to institutionalize. It would be desirable for a congregation to develop a certain amount of familiarity with the writings in the sociology—and the political science—of organizations, several of which have been listed in the notes to this chapter and chapter 3. Only thus will a congregation be able to develop a balanced appreciation of the implications of its ministerial choices.

7

The Seed

What model, or combination of models, would be best for religious congregations after the year 2000—now less than a decade away? Some congregations may adopt a purely associational form, organized around societal or spiritual goals and similar to Pax Christi or parish-based prayer groups such as the Renew program. For these congregations, very little effort or planning will be needed, either by the leadership or by the members, to coordinate the emergence of their new form. Indeed, many congregations appear to be drifting toward associational lifestyles without any planning whatever. In my studies of changes in living patterns among women religious in the United States during the past twenty-five years, I have found that the median size of the groups in which sisters live has decreased from eight or nine in 1964 to one or two today. This means that, among women religious not living in their order's motherhouse or infirmary, a large proportion—sometimes the majority—are living either alone or with only one other person. In some congregational directories, almost two-thirds of the addresses are of individuals living alone in apartments, and fewer than twenty percent of the entries are identifiable as convents. Women religious rarely return to communal living after the experience of living alone. While I have no comparable data on the living patterns of male religious communities, Arbuckle appears to be describing an associational, "gentlemen's club" lifestyle among them as well, even when they still physically reside under the same roof.[1] The current trend seems to be for religious congregations to move increasingly toward the kind of living arrangements that are most typical of associational, rather than communal, commitment.

Although they may require no assistance in their transition, associational congregations *will* need help in finding a focus for their existence that will be sufficiently attractive to draw new members. The field of competing associations, both spiritually- and socially-oriented, is already rather crowded, and it will be necessary for the congregation to find its "ecological niche" in the field: some unique need to be met or resource to be offered which is currently unfilled. If it finds such a niche, the associational congregation will also need help in advertising itself to potential members, and in overcoming some of the obstacles to associational recruitment listed in chapter 5. Associations must give potential members concrete reasons for joining them, and former intentional communities usually lack both the vocabulary and the practical experience for this task. The difficulty that intentional communities have in attracting new members or retaining their old ones after they become associations is evidenced by the fact that such groups rarely if ever survive.[2] Current indications seem to portend a similar demise for those religious congregations who choose, or drift into, a largely associational model.

A congregation may, of course, deliberately *choose* to die. Unlike bureaucratic organizations, which never choose their own death,[3] most religious congregations still retain some communitarian characteristics. And members of intentional communities often prefer to dissolve their group rather than commit their energy and resources to goals on which they do not all agree. This tendency deliberately to choose death is one reason why intentional communities are usually short-lived, and is, I suspect, the explanation for why so many religious congregations die out at the end of each cycle of religious life rather than refound themselves. All available sociological evidence indicates that only those intentional communities which retain their commitment mechanisms survive. But if the members disagree either on the value of these commitment mechanisms or on the ideology which lies

behind them, the group is quite likely to choose death rather than
to continue such practices. This is also a reason why charismatic
founders, when they do arise, generally begin new intentional
communities rather than attempt to refound an already-
existing one.

The third alternative—and the only one likely to lead to
congregational survival—is to retain or readopt at least some
intentional community commitment mechanisms. Commitment,
however, cannot be imposed from above. The members of most
congregations now have widely diverse interpretations of their
community's founding charism, as well as varying degrees of
commitment to it:

> In some congregations this pluralism has become so great that
> it is difficult to see what remains in common in any vital
> sense. Members have some vague sense of belonging to a
> group. This sense of belonging is usually sustained by a vague
> ethos or spirit, by memories of a shared history, by a sense of
> responsibility for the elderly members and by personal rela-
> tionships with those who are co-workers, co-inhabitants, or
> like-minded allies. *But belonging is not the same as commit-
> ment.*[4] [italics in original]

In congregations whose members possess divergent interpretations of their founding charism, it is impossible for the governing
council or even for the congregational chapter/assembly to legis-
late any return to a common level of ideological commitment,
much less to prescribe the mechanisms that would foster and
maintain this level. Any attempts to do so would be extremely
divisive and, probably, ignored. So chapters and assemblies avoid
addressing the issue in any but the most general terms. Leddy lists
some patterns of action which emerge as a congregation tries to
operate "in the absence of a vital and common sense of meaning:"

1. Statements of mission or charism which are vague and
   general enough to include all the various interests in a
   congregation.

2. Difficulty in making choices, particularly in the area of long-term planning, because there is no deeply shared vision upon which to base these choices.

3. An emphasis on the personal growth and development of the members. A tendency to interpret community in terms of the needs of the members, work as an individual project and spirituality as a private concern.

4. The near impossibility of sustaining corporate commitments.

5. An increasing difficulty in finding persons for leadership positions.[5]

There are more examples in Leddy's list, but the ones quoted here are sufficient to make the point. *However vital for their future it may be to do so, congregations cannot and will not impose commitment-enhancing practices upon their members.*

But, in most cases, the individual members are unable to adopt such commitment practices on their own initiative, or at least to continue them in any sustained fashion. In the past decade or so, many small sub-groups of four to six religious have joined together to live a more intense or personally fulfilling common life, voluntarily imposing upon themselves a set of specific time commitments to group activities, a more rigorous standard of common prayer, a simpler way of living, or similar obligations.[6] In the course of one or several years, however, these groups usually disband. In some, the members find that they possess varying and divisive interpretations of their commitment to the group. Other groups, in the increased intensity of their common life, uncover psychologically addictive or co-dependent patterns in some of their members, patterns that had perhaps remained hidden in larger groups or when the members had been living alone. In still other groups, natural changes in ministry, family commitments, study leaves and the like lead to the break-up of the group. And the few groups which do manage to avoid all these pitfalls and to survive for longer than five or six years often became quite stable in their membership. The research I have done on congregational living patterns, in addition to showing the trend toward single living that I mentioned above, also shows a vastly increased degree of stability in the composition of larger houses. In some congregations, as many as ninety percent of the local living groups experience no change in membership from one year to the next. No matter how beautifully a small group may have recommitted itself to a more intense level of community living, if its membership remains unchanged for five or ten years, new members will hesitate to join them.

The result of these tendencies is that even those religious who might prefer to live a more communal life may find themselves living alone anyway. It is difficult for an individual religious to organize an intentionally communal group of four to six individuals on his/her own initiative, and so the number of such groups in any given congregation will be few. An individual who may wish to participate in a more communal style of religious life may find that the one opportunity for doing so is full, or else may be intimidated by the prospect of joining a "clique" of people who have all lived together for a very long time. Furthermore, the members currently living in a communal group may have no similar group to move to if their own group ever dissolves.

We thus appear to have arrived at an impasse, where all of the alternatives open to a religious congregation are unfeasible or undesirable or both. Religious communities may continue their drift toward an associational model, which has not been a viable alternative for the other intentional communities that took this route in the past. Or they can choose to die. Or they can rekindle a greater and more universal level of commitment in their members—a feat which is impossibly divisive when initiated from the top down, and doomed to eventual failure when initiated from the bottom up. Are there no other alternatives? Must a religious community's survival wait for charismatic refounders who may never arise, and whose message would split any existing congregation in two if they did?

A basic point of this book has been that, by the creative and informed addition of sociological insights to the theological and psychological studies which have already been done on religious life, such alternatives can be found. The needs and potentialities of the communitarian, bureaucratic and associational elements of religious communities can be taken into account and actively used in modeling the religious life of the future. I would like to offer a parable illustrating one way in which this adaptation might be done—the parable of the seed.

"The sower went out to sow" (Mk 4:4)

Religious congregations and their leadership cannot *impose* commitment. But they can *facilitate* the coming together of any small groups among their members who may wish to develop and live a more communal life. Through certain concrete actions, congregations can actively assist these individuals in overcoming the obstacles which have so often led to the demise of similar groups. I use the image of the congregation as "sower" here: both the congregation's leadership and its members would act together to sow "seeds" of small intentional communities and communitarian/associational mixtures. No congregational member would be required to join such a group. In fact, there would probably be many individuals within the sowing congregation who would continue to live alone and maintain a more associational style of membership. But voluntarily communal living groups are difficult to form and sustain when only the individuals personally involved in them are working for their existence. Congregational facilitation by the leadership and by the independently-living associational members would be necessary in order to ensure that those who wished to follow such a communitarian model had the means to do so. In the long run, the presence and growth of the voluntarily communitarian sector of a congregation might also aid in the survival of its associational religious lifestyle. While intentional communities that become completely associational in form do not survive, religious communities which develop associational branches ("Third Orders," in the language of a former era) often thrive. Many newly founded and flourishing groups—the

Italian Comunione e Liberazione and the French Chemin Neuf community, for example—offer their members the option of participating either associationally or communally in the life of the group.[7] Even if many religious have no intention ever to submit again to the vicissitudes of communal group living, it will still be to their advantage to help the others among their fellow members who wish to do so.

How might a congregation facilitate the sowing and the continued growth of communitarian "seed" groups—the seeds around which their future form may develop in the coming sixth era of religious life? On the practical level, a congregation would first have to take steps to ensure that adequate physical space is available for such groups to live in. In most parts of the country, it is rare to find apartments with more than two bedrooms, and houses with more than three bedrooms are also scarce. Neither would be adequate for a group of four to eight religious who wished to live communally. Elsewhere[8] I have detailed some of the reasons why four is the minimal size for such a group. It is sufficient here to say simply that sociological research has found groups of two to be excessively stable over time—independently of any personal or psychological characteristics of the individuals involved—and to resist the introduction of a third member. This tendency is exacerbated by the fact that the triad is an extremely unstable form which frequently suffers splits, coalitions, and other types of divisive interactions between its members. If a religious community relies on housing available in the mainstream housing market, therefore, it is likely to find its members relegated to living singly or in very stable pairs. Once aware of this possibly unintended consequence, a congregational chapter or assembly might decide to ensure that larger facilities are made available. This could be done by purchasing or renting unused parish convents, if they are of the appropriate size. Or some congregations might consider purchasing an abandoned and tax-delinquent two-family building at a city auction, and renovating it for communal living. Other possibilities will doubtless occur to the reader. The important thing is that, when a group of religious discerns a call to join together in some more communitarian life-style, sufficient facilities need to be available to house them.

A second way a congregation could facilitate the sowing of these new seeds of community life would be to coordinate the use of whatever living facilities they have purchased, rented, or developed for this purpose. The congregation, or perhaps a group of congregations in a city, could devise and initiate a process for matching prospective groups with available houses. For example, an applying group might be requested to specify their mission or purpose for coming together, the level of their communal commitment to each other, and the way that the daily living out of this commitment would take place. After a few years, as those facilitating this application process gained experience, they might be able to take a more active role in helping the applying groups— suggesting practices that have worked for others, for example, or pitfalls to be avoided. Another service which this intra- or inter-congregational facilitation process might render would be to advertise openings as they became available in the communitarian groups, to assist individuals seeking such a group in their discernment process, and to walk with established groups in their reception and integration of new members.

It may occur to some readers that the process described in the preceding paragraph sounds like the addition of another layer of bureaucratic offices and procedures. To some extent, this may be unavoidable, because applying groups will expect the sort of universal and clearly articulated application and evaluation procedures that bureaucratic standards supply. But the limitations of the bureaucratic form should always be kept in mind. A "sowing" congregation is trying to facilitate the establishment and growth of groups with a wide variety of creative combinations of new commitment mechanisms, with mixtures of associational and communitarian features, and with new ministerial foci. To reject an applying group because of the over-rigid application of bureaucratic standards would be a tragedy. Whatever congregational

offices or committees develop to coordinate the application process for its communal houses should act more as facilitators and
nurturers than as impartial bureaucracies.

A final function which a congregation could perform in the
sowing process is to help communitarian living groups in their
inevitable times of strain and transition. Trained facilitators could
be made available to the groups at these times to assist members if
varied interpretations of their commitment obligations are caus-
ing stress and misunderstanding, or if deep psychological bro-
kenness surfaces in some individual and becomes detrimental to
group functioning. Since these kinds of strain are inevitable in all
small communitarian groups, a congregation might even consider
making the regular use of a facilitator one of the prerequisites for
accepting a group's application in the first place. In developing
the role of facilitators, great care would have to be taken to avoid
slipping back into the "decoupled," ceremonialized style of community evaluation described in chapter 3, where the most important strains in the group are not addressed. As an outside and
neutral observer/mediator, the facilitator would have to be able to
ask challenging questions and point out any evasions in the an-
swers. If it actually became necessary for a small group to dissolve, the congregational facilitators could assist the members in
finding more satisfactory situations—whether alone or in another
group—and could help a new community to form.

"Unless the seed dies . . ." (Jn 12:24)

Actually, seeds are not supposed to die. By its very nature,
each seed carries within itself a spark of life that is meant to live
and grow. What a seed *does* do, however, is separate from the
mother plant to live and grow on its own. Many, if not most, seeds
do not survive the separation process—they may fall in inhospita-
ble soil by the wayside or among choking thorns. The mother
plant produces many seeds in order that a few, at least, will fall on
good soil and produce a hundredfold. Similarly, the goal of a

sowing congregation should be to foster as many small communitarian living groups as its members are willing to try, and, eventually, to encourage their independent growth. The majority of the seeds a congregation sows will die. They will not attract new entrants; their particular amalgam of community-enhancing practices, or their philosophy/ideology, or their mission vis-a-vis the larger society will not "click" with the needs of that society;[9] they will succumb to the many strains of living together that afflict any intentional community. As Hostie has pointed out, many founders of religious communities had to go through an apprenticeship of several failed attempts, learning each time from the experience, before they hit upon the right combination for their era.[10] In the same way, there will be a high mortality rate among the seed communities until one or a few accidentally stumble upon a combination that works in the twenty-first century. It is the role of the religious congregation in this process to encourage the sowing (and the nurturing) of as many seed communities as possible, in as wide a variety as possible, and in as many settings as possible—over and over and over again, despite repeated failures, in the hope of a harvest that the current members may never see. It only takes one surviving seed, however slow in germination, to produce a hundredfold. Actively sowing small communal groups may require more faith in the future than continuing passively in the status quo and assuming that somehow things will work out. The most that such a passive strategy would be likely to achieve for a congregation would be what Chittister calls a level of "minimal survival," basically irrelevant to the church and society, while the prophetic charism of religious life moves elsewhere.[11] A more likely alternative is congregational death, and a death without the hope of resurrection which the sowing strategy offers.

After facilitating the formation of a wide variety of small communal groups, a congregation must also work for their independent growth and operation. This is necessary because the order is trying to facilitate the birth of what will be, in many respects, a new daughter congregation—its communal embodiment in the coming age of religious life and the nucleus around which its associational members can gather. In order to achieve this independence, the congregation may have to allow or even require financial self-sufficiency of its germinating seed. This could perhaps be coupled with a safety net for the care of retired or ill religious (who might then rejoin the larger congregation or else continue living in the smaller group), and with some provision for the members of communitarian groups that split up. While these interdependent links between the sowing congregation and its seed may endure for a long time, ultimately the new group will have to pull its own weight.

The seed analogy also implies eventual *recruitment independence* on the part of the smaller group. This means that the members of a small communitarian seed community must accept a twofold responsibility for attracting others to join them. Each local member should be expected, first of all, to invite persons not of the congregation to become associated with their life and, ultimately, to become full members of the group. The larger congregation could facilitate this task in several ways. It could require an outreach aspect to be a specifically-outlined part of every potential group's application process before they could be accepted for one of the congregation's housing facilities. Whether or not the outreach plans were followed would then become a part of the group's self-evaluation process, shared with the congregational facilitation team. A congregation might even consider initiating a set of quasi-independent formation programs, whereby small groups that are successful at attracting new members will also live with those they attract and even plan and supervise their formation. If this particular small communitarian living group is to be the seed of the future congregational form, it must be able to be self-sufficient in membership recruitment and retention, as well as in finances.

The second implication of an independent recruitment responsibility is the attraction of new small group members from within the larger congregation. Sociologically speaking, it is not a good idea for the same five or six individuals to live together in the same small intentional community for the rest of their lives.

The members themselves may come to need the distance of a more associational lifestyle after a time, and may benefit by moving out of the group. Also, after a few years, the insular "in-group" characteristics which long-term residents acquire will deter anyone else from joining them. Such a stable group would never grow beyond its original members, and thus could never serve as a seed for the future. Congregations might choose to purchase or provide several communitarian houses at the same time, and then encourage (or even require) the individual religious living there to move on after a given number of years. As they left, these religious might move into another communitarian house or into single apartment living. Other ways might also be devised whereby a healthy turnover and the infusion of "fresh blood" could be encouraged in the local communitarian groups sponsored by the sowing congregation. If maintaining a sufficient number of houses for this type of mobility is beyond the financial or personnel means of a single community, ways of pooling resources with other congregations in the same tradition (other Dominicans, other Franciscans, etc.), or even with congregations in other traditions, might be explored. Another possible way to achieve sufficient turnover (and to attract more new members from outside the order) might be to admit lay members for a temporary commitment only. Some recent studies of young people have indicated that they would be more willing to join a religious community on a temporary rather than a permanent basis,[12] and many of the most successful new and established religious groups actively promote temporary membership.[13]

Whatever arrangements a "sowing" congregation makes to encourage the development and the gradual independence of a wide variety of seed communities, it will be obvious when one succeeds. In previous eras of religious life, the successful new forms characteristically attracted many adherents. If a small intentional community within a congregation develops a style of living and a spirituality that fits the current needs of the people of God, it will grow, perhaps quite rapidly. The parent congregation may facilitate this stage by locating additional living facilities for the growing group, or the seed community may expand on its own. This may be a stressful time both for the sowing congregation and its growing seed, for the new group's interpretation of the congregational charism may have been transformed and no longer be quite the same as that of the other members of the congregation. Some of these other members may even disagree profoundly with the new interpretation of their charism, and may resent the utilization of congregational resources to support such a deviant group—one which has become all the more threatening now that it seems to be succeeding. Some small seed groups, for example, may have adopted charismatic prayer styles that make other members uncomfortable, or may even be perceived as "cult-like" by some in the larger group. If tension increases, the seed community may eventually split off totally, or it may continue in a looser federation with its parent congregation. The working out of the legal and financial details in either case would be complex and perhaps painful.

God gives each seed its own sort of body (1 Cor 15:38)

What will the successful seed communities be like? Predicting the future is a notoriously imprecise business, as the congregational leaders who built large novitiates in the early 1960s for the hundreds of anticipated Baby Boom entrants can testify. Any attempt to outline the kinds of communities which will arise in the sixth era of religious life will probably contain more inaccuracy than prophecy. Still, whatever form the new communitarian religious life takes, it will arise in the context of North American (or Latino, or European, or Asian, or African) culture in the twenty-first century. "The institutional form the vowed life takes in each historical era rises out of the major structural strains of that era."[14] Even counter-cultural groups must be "counter" to a specific culture, and are thus defined by their opposition to it.

> Structures which resist larger, encompassing structures through opposition and separation, nevertheless themselves repeat the forms of these structures. . . . The kind of organic self-sufficiency, by virtue of which the same stream of life flows through all group members, is borrowed by the group from the larger whole, to whose forms the members had been adapted. The smaller structure can meet this whole most viably, precisely by imitating it.[15]

While much of the current decline of religious life is due to the dropping of communitarian commitment mechanisms and the pitfalls of moving to an associational model, much is also due to the fact that pre-Vatican II religious life was responding to a culture that no longer existed. Congregations cannot go back to the old model. They must arise anew in response to the needs of today's society.

Where, then, are the structural strains and needs in current, post-industrial American culture? A prime area of strain is the need for spirituality, for prayer, for a sense of transcendent meaning to one's life beyond the siren song of success and wealth. "What has dropped out are the old normative expectations of what makes life worth living."[16] In my first years of college teaching, I taught at a small Presbyterian college with an active women's spirituality group. I was amazed by the spiritual searching of these young women—one had spent time in Taizé, another's daily schedule included an hour of mental prayer. All expressed regret upon graduating that they would no longer have a group with which they could share their prayer life. Similar hungers are widespread in our culture, and are usually met by extremely fundamentalist groups in both the Protestant and Catholic traditions—a distressing prospect for women, since fundamentalism often contains sexist overtones. For Catholic Americans, the general spiritual hunger discussed here is exacerbated by the decline of the parish as a focus and wellspring for their spiritual life. The situation will worsen as fewer and fewer priests are stretched increasingly thin, for most parishes and dioceses do not yield sufficient authority to lay leaders that would enable them to address the spiritual needs even of active Catholics.

Another need in American Catholicism, which springs from this same strain of religious hunger in the larger American society, is the need to reach out to Catholics who are largely isolated from the church's message. This includes, first of all, young Catholics in their teens and early twenties. The majority of these show an appalling lack of knowledge of even the basic elements of their faith,[17] and are, moreover, the group most estranged from the church.[18] Studies have shown that the single most critical factor in how close young Catholics feel to the church is their experience of their local parish,[19] a finding that, when combined with the aging of church personnel and the merging of parishes into larger and more impersonal entities, does not bode well for the possibility of future improvement along this line.

Other alienated Catholics whose spiritual hungers could be better addressed by the church include the Baby Boom generation, now in their thirties and early forties. While studies have found a "modest" rebound in religious activity among this age cohort as they marry and begin to raise their own families, a good many of them still remain uninvolved in the religion of their youth.[20] Another group, which this book has already mentioned, are Latinos, whose isolation from leadership opportunities in an Anglo-dominated church has resulted in a high conversion rate to various Protestant sects.[21] Still another category might be Catholic intellectuals, and more educated Catholics in general.

A prime structural strain in American society, therefore, and one which will undoubtedly influence the orientation and vision of many new forms of religious life, is a hunger and need for spirituality, which is often not met by the organized church today. Congregations in the Benedictine and Dominican traditions might be the most advantageously placed to develop new ways to address this strain. There are other strains as well, however. I will suggest three, which might also serve as foci for new seed communities. There is, first of all, a need to articulate and model a

spirituality and a praxis that address the ecological interrela-
tionships of our society. Some work along this line has already
been done:

> At the very time when the Charismatic Renewal was spread-
> ing, certain groups of young intellectuals were being affected
> by another wave of "sacrality." It went by the name of ecol-
> ogy—not ecology in the ordinary limited sense, but a verita-
> ble mystique of ecology, a mystique that was altogether secu-
> lar for many, but religious in the case of others. The challenge
> of these people to the productivistic society of the organiza-
> tion came, above all, from their opposition to the destruction
> being wrought in the "ecosystem," the damage done to the
> balance normally to be found in nature. In some cases, this
> challenge had an apocalyptic tinge about it which led the
> persons concerned to leave the "world" and find refuge in the
> "desert." Some "new beginnings" have their origin in this
> "return to nature."[22]

Perhaps new forms of religious life will develop to enflesh the
ecological model of stewarding creation. Some version of the
Franciscan charism would seem especially suited to this.

Another structural strain is the split between the wealthy
countries of the northern hemisphere and the increasingly impoverished and indebted southern hemisphere. This north/south polarization is likely to become more intense as preoccupation with
the communist/non-communist rift recedes from western consciousness. Already, African countries have expressed a concern,
echoed by John Paul II, that aid to reconstruct the economies of
eastern Europe will divert needed funds from their own plight.[23]
In the "developed" countries as well, the gap between rich and
poor is widening. A prime focus of current religious orders such
as Maryknoll and the Central American Jesuits has been to stand
in solidarity with the poor; this stance will increase in importance.
Small communal groups in the Mercy and Charity traditions,
among others, have already begun experimenting with new ways
of standing with the poor in this country. Whether the focus is on

domestic or on third world poverty, the challenge for emerging religious communities will be to articulate and practice this stand in ways that most truly touch and challenge both rich and poor.

A final source of structural strain, in American society and throughout the world, is the need for empowering women and admitting them into the public, "central" institutions of society. Even constituencies of women who do not self-consciously identify themselves as feminist express a growing consciousness of the ways that they are disenfranchised.[24] In American Catholicism, especially, the exclusion of women from full participation in the structures and the spirituality of the church bids fair to lose the allegiance of an entire generation.[25] Communal groups of women religious might be able to offer valuable and empowering alternatives to these women.

The successful seed communities will thus be the ones which somehow offer a viable and attractive and *lived* answer to structural strains such as these in their surrounding society. It will not be enough, however, for a community to focus on one of these cultural strains; *the day-to-day organization of the community's commitment-enhancing mechanisms must also be congruent with their culture.* The development of new commitment practices will be difficult, because, as chapter 5 pointed out, our previous commitment mechanisms were modeled largely on the European monastic model and were profoundly antithetical to many deeply-held American values. And American culture lacks even a vocabulary to express the need for commitment to a transcendent good:

> The notion that one discovers one's deepest beliefs in, and through, tradition and community is not very congenial to Americans. Most of us imagine an autonomous self existing independently, entirely outside any tradition and community, and then perhaps choosing one.[26]

This is another reason for sowing a wide variety of seed communities and for encouraging, at least initially, frequent changes of personnel among them: such creative ferment will make it more likely that some group, somewhere, will stumble upon culturally-congruent commitment mechanisms which have not existed so far, and which we lack even the vocabulary to describe.[27] Successful small intentional communities, therefore, will have to devise new ways of celebrating their founding world view in ritual, of encouraging togetherness through common activities among their members, of insulating themselves from competing value systems, and of harnessing—in a psychologically healthy manner—the tremendously powerful forces of sacrifice and self-denial.[28] When one of the seed communities does stumble upon a set of commitment-enhancing practices that fit with American culture, it will most likely grow quite rapidly.

Most of this section, so far, has been theoretical and general. I would like to conclude by offering some concrete examples of the kinds of possible seed communities that could be developed by congregations, modeled on flourishing new communal and communal-associational groups which a recent study has described in Europe.[29] It is possible that none of the examples listed here will prove to be successful. It is also quite likely that various permutations of them already exist in this country. They are listed here merely in order to spark brainstorming sessions among interested religious, and to encourage the creation of a wide variety of modifications and additions—varying from each other in their setting, in their focus, in their commitment requirements, and in their day-to-day practices—in the hope that one out of all the variations developed by the sowing congregations will prove to be the seed that grows and yields fruit in the sixth era of religious life.

Seed Phylum A: Meeting Spiritual Hungers

Several different forms and styles of small, voluntarily communal religious groups might be envisioned that would address the spiritual hunger in American society. A small communal group might model itself on the Citadins of Paris, who, although they work part-time at a variety of secular jobs, have as their primary aim being present in the heart of the city and celebrating the liturgy and divine office with the townspeople in the most inspiring manner possible. A recent description of their services, crowded with the young and the old from all walks of life, makes it evident that they are meeting a felt need.[30] While the group describes itself as "monastic," Swift's account shows the many adaptations they have made to the traditional monastic commitment mechanisms in order to fit them to their mission in the contemporary world.

A possible setting for a group with a similar lifestyle and mission might be in an unused parish convent or rectory, especially in those parts of the country where the growing priest shortage might mean that no regular parish priest was available. As with the Citadins, community participants might work in other jobs but devote their primary energies to developing good prayer experiences, on a daily basis, for the parish. For obvious reasons, this setting would probably work only if there was no priest in the parish, or if the priest was himself a community member. Also, the model assumes a considerable amount of musical and artistic ability, and liturgical expertise, on the part of the community members.

A parish might also serve as the setting for another type of small intentional community, this one with its mission focused on improving the ways in which the parish could address more of the needs of its people. Whether the community members all worked at jobs elsewhere or were employed by the parish itself would vary from group to group among the intentional communities following this model. Some permutations of inside vs. outside employment would turn out to work more smoothly than others. But all the members would commit themselves to working actively, for a significant amount of time each week, to further the life of the parish. One member might develop, for example, an active youth program, while another organized an adult Bible study group, led or sang in the choir, visited shut-ins, or whatever. As with the Citadins, the success of this type of group will depend on whether it fills a felt need, and also on the commitment of its members, sustained and enhanced by carefully adapted and applied commitment mechanisms.

Seed Phylum B: Solidarity with the Poor

There are at least two possible ways of addressing the challenge posed by the growing split between the rich and the poor in our country and the world, each of which may be developed into a wide variety of unique lifestyles for small intentional communities. One way is for religious to choose to live with the poor, as they live, in the decaying urban and rural areas of our country. "They positively concern themselves with the really poor of our affluent society, intent not so much on sharing their misery—that would be a delusion—as on standing by them in their struggles for justice and being the kind of person to be counted on by those who are of no account to anybody."[31] A group's members might choose to live in an impoverished area while working elsewhere, and to involve themselves actively in becoming friends with their neighbors, listening to their stories, and fighting their battles— against drugs, slum landlords, etc.—in solidarity with them. A second way would be exemplified by a group of religious who came together to operate some specific ministry to the poor: to run a shelter for the homeless or for battered women, for example, or a nursery for abandoned AIDS babies. Some groups may combine these two foci in various ways. Others may develop creative ways of organizing both live-in communal members and more associational member-employees together around the work. Quite a few groups in these categories are already flourishing in inner city and rural areas. It would be helpful if opportunities were provided for them to share their successes and failures with each other, and with others who might wish to begin a similar lifestyle.

A problem which Hostie has observed in all religious orders with a primarily ministerial focus is that they usually last only as long as the need they were created to meet.[32] However, since the gap between rich and poor seems likely to persist for a long time, this is a valid and enduring base for newly-forming, small intentional communities of religious. Six of the thirty-three new religious communities cited by *Pro Mundi Vita* had some ministerial focus on the poor or neglected of society. One group, the community of San Egidio, actively welcomes as members the poor among whom it ministers:

> What is still more striking and original is the fact that often the community does not act on behalf of persons who are victims of city life, but rather makes them its own—there are hundreds of young workers or young people who are members of the community, hundreds from secondary or vocational schools who, equally with the adults, share in this community's openness which draws them out of abandonment and isolation.[33]

Seed Phylum C: Stewarding the Earth

While a desire to live lightly on the land and to steward God's creation has often been the impetus for founding secular communal groups, there are fewer intentional communities within Roman Catholic religious life for whom this has been a primary focus. Still, it would not be impossible to envision a small community group which devoted itself to reclaiming strip-mined land in a rural Appalachian county, or to developing community gardens in rubble-strewn inner city lots. In my own congregation, there is a sister who has built a solar house almost entirely of recycled materials in an abandoned farm building on the motherhouse property, and who is actively involved in developing and sharing a spirituality oriented toward ecological awareness.[34]

Seed Phylum D: Toward a Non-Sexist Society[35]

Small communal groups of women religious would seem especially well-suited to develop new ways of countering patriarchal structures of domination in all aspects of our society. Their previous experiences with weak tie networking, mentoring, running large institutions and devising non-bureaucratic forms of leadership would all be valuable and valued contributions to the efforts of women everywhere in creating a society and a church with equal opportunity for all. Other seed groups in this category might focus on developing non-sexist worship rituals accessible to the women—and men—in their local parish or neighborhood (a hybrid with seed phylum A). Again, there are undoubtedly small intentional communities around the country which are already doing this in some form, and more opportunities should be created for them to share their experiences with others who are interested in beginning similar groups.

> While the "seed community" would within itself be conscious of issues of domination, their ministry would be precisely an awareness that relationships of domination and submission are both personal and political, and [they would] work toward transforming those relationships. Whether the focus among women's communities would be linked to the issues raised by Women-Church, or "organizing" in the business world, or in governmental and political agencies, the vision would be Galatians 3:28–29 and a response to the forces of domination and division, whether expressed in terms of class, race, nation or gender.[36]

Seed Phylum E: Community as a Value in Itself

Several—in fact, the plurality—of the new religious groups which have recently been founded have focused on the common life as a value in itself. An example is the Nikola-Kommunauteit in the Netherlands: "The ideal they all earnestly pursue is to take the Gospel seriously, to pool resources, to pray, to be open to the needs of others, to devote themselves more and more to being available to and serving others."[37] In this country, the "New Jerusalem" community in Cincinnati, Ohio appears to be one expression of this type of group.[38] There are many others as well, each enfleshing this goal in a different combination of associational or communitarian lifestyles, religious or lay membership, temporary or permanent commitment. Some of the new seed communities begun by religious congregations may likewise have a variety of ministerial works or even of ideological/philosophical beliefs (the thirty members of Nikola-Kommunauteit belong to three different Christian denominations), but be united by their commitment to an intense common life.

Conclusion

There are still many other foci for seed communities—living with and ministering to college students, for example, or working with drug addicts, or developing American Catholic intellectual life through writing, study and research. There are also many permutations of the ways in which the communitarian membership can be linked with the associational membership, and many, many healthy ways in which a group's members could celebrate and strengthen their commitment to each other and to their founding ideology. The important thing is that the seed and the seedling are images of growth and of hope in the future, through which, I believe, all the members of a congregation could move actively into the coming age of religious life. This book has been a call to each religious who reads it—whether in leadership or not, whether committed apartment dweller living alone or equally committed member of a seed community itself, whether current member or ex-member or future member of whatever congregation—to lend active support to the sowing in his/her own way. Religious life has had twenty-five years of dying. It is time again for sowing, for rebirth, for growth.

What is the reign of God like?
What parable can we find for it?
It is like a mustard seed, when sown the smallest of seeds.
Night and day, while you sleep, while you wake,
it sprouts and grows,
how, you do not know.
When grown, it becomes a tree,
and the birds of the air can shelter in its shade.
(see Mk 4:26–32)

Notes

1. INTRODUCTION

1. Benjamin Zablocki, *Alienation and Charisma: A Study of Contemporary American Communes* (New York: Free Press, 1980), Chapter 1.

2. Hugh Gardner, *The Children of Prosperity* (New York: St. Martin's Press, 1978), pp. 15–20.

3. See Rosabeth M. Kanter, *Men and Women of the Corporation* (New York: Basic Books, 1977), chapters 3 and 5.

4. This is also true for politicians and their wives. Recently a Cleveland newspaper ran an editorial complaining that the governor's wife, Dagmar Celeste, did not behave like one: she wore blue jeans, for example, and supported controversial causes. Joan Kennedy, Margaret Trudeau and Kitty Dukakis are other examples of how wives are affected when the private lives of top governmental executives come under scrutiny.

5. Lewis Coser, *Greedy Institutions: Patterns of Undivided Commitment* (New York: Free Press, 1974), pp. 119–126. Erving Goffman's *Asylums* (Chicago: Aldine, 1961) makes passing mention of monasteries and convents in its discussion of total institutions, but, as Goffman himself admitted, his observations were not intended to apply to religious life. (See Goffman's letter to Sr. Miriam, O.S.U., in Kathleen M. Cooney, "Reasons for Staying in a Religious Congregation from the Viewpoint of Women Who

Entered Between 1945 and 1965." Ph.D. Dissertation, Case Western University, 1988. Appendix B, p. 379.)

6. *Signs*, vol. 10, no. 4 (Summer 1985).

7. Ruby Rohrlich and E.H. Baruch, *Women in Search of Utopia: Mavericks and Mythmakers* (New York: Schocken Books, 1984); Sally L. Kitch, *Chaste Liberation: Celibacy and Female Cultural Status* (Urbana: University of Illinois Press, 1989).

8. Some of these include Dean R. Hoge, *The Future of Catholic Leadership* (Kansas City: Sheed and Ward, 1987), Joseph H. Fichter, *The Organization Man in the Church* (Cambridge: Schenkman, 1974), Fred H. Gouldner, "The Production of Cynical Knowledge in Organizations," *American Sociological Review*, vol. 42 (1977), pp. 539–551, and Douglas T. Hall and Benjamin Schneider, *Organizational Climates and Careers: The Work Lives of Priests* (New York: Seminar Press, 1973).

9. Helen R.F. Ebaugh, *Out of the Cloister: A Study of Organizational Dilemmas* (Austin: University of Texas Press, 1977).

10. J. Miller McPherson and Lynn Smith-Lovin, "Women and Weak Ties: Differences by Sex in the Size of Voluntary Organizations," *American Journal of Sociology*, vol. 87 (1982) pp. 883–904.

11. Herbert Gans, "Sociology in America: The Discipline and the Public," *American Sociological Review*, vol. 54 (1989), pp. 8–9.

12. Gerald A. Arbuckle, S.M., *Out of Chaos: Refounding Religious Congregations* (New York: Paulist Press, 1988), p. 1.

13. Bennett M. Berger, *The Survival of a Counterculture* (Berkeley: University of California Press, 1981), p. 184.

14. William J. Barry, S.J., "Are Social Scientists Authorities on Morality?" *Human Development*, vol. 10 (Summer 1989), p. 25.

2. INTENTIONAL COMMUNITIES AND RELIGIOUS LIFE

1. Patricia Wittberg "Transformations in Religious Commitment," *Review for Religious*, vol. 44, no. 2 (1985), p. 161. This

sociological definition is different from the usage in Bernard Lee's and Michael Cowan's *Dangerous Memories* (Kansas City: Sheed and Ward, 1986), which employs the term to refer to home-based churches. It is also slightly different from an emerging use among religious congregations, where "intentional community" often refers to small voluntary living groups within the larger community. These local groups may possess many characteristics similar to sociological intentional communities, or they may not. If they do, they will impact on the larger congregation in several key ways. Chapter 7 will explore some of them.

2. See Erving Goffman, "The Characteristics of Total Institutions," pp. 319–339, in Amitai Etzioni and Edward Lehman, eds., *A Sociological Reader on Complex Organizations* (New York: Holt, Rinehart and Winston, 1980).

3. James R. Lewis, "Apostates and the Legitimation of Repression: Some Historical and Empirical Perspectives on the Cult Controversy," *Sociological Analysis*, vol. 49, no. 4 (1989) p. 386, explicitly compares attempts to extricate present-day cult members with the efforts by distraught parents in previous decades to persuade their children to leave religious life.

4. Rosabeth M. Kanter, *Commitment and Community: Communes and Utopias in Sociological Perspective* (Cambridge: Harvard University Press, 1972), p. 32.

5. Benjamin Zablocki, *The Joyful Community* (Chicago: University of Chicago Press, 1980), p. 160.

6. Robert Bellah et al., *Habits of the Heart* (New York: Harper and Row, 1985).

7. This section is an adaptation of Kanter, op. cit., pp. 64–106.

8. Max Weber, "The Sociology of Charismatic Authority," pp. 245–52, in H.H. Gerth and C. Wright Mills, eds., *From Max Weber: Essays in Sociology* (New York: Oxford University Press, 1958).

9. Lawrence Veysey, *The Communal Experience* (Chicago: University of Chicago Press, 1973), p. 273.

10. Edward A. Wynne, *Traditional Catholic Religious Orders: Living in Community* (New Brunswick: Transaction, 1988), p.

76. See also Roy Wallis, *The Elementary Forms of the New Religious Life* (London: Routledge and Kegan Paul, 1984), chapter 7.

11. John Lofland, "White Hot Mobilization: Strategies of a Millenarian Movement," pp. 157–66, in Mayer N. Zald and John D. McCarthy, eds., *The Dynamics of Social Movements* (Cambridge: Winthrop Publishers, 1979).

12. Wynne, op. cit., p. 76.

13. Wallis, op. cit., Chapter 7.

14. Barry Shenker, *Intentional Communities: Ideology and Alienation in Communal Societies* (London: Routledge and Kegan Paul, 1986), p. 71.

15. Benjamin Zablocki, *Alienation and Charisma: A Study of Contemporary American Communes* (New York: Free Press, 1980), p. 128.

16. Shenker, op. cit., p. 142.

17. Zablocki, *Alienation and Charisma*, op. cit., p. 10.

18. Thomas Luckmann, quoted in Lawrence Cada et al., *Shaping the Coming Age of Religious Life* (New York: Seabury Press, 1979), p. 95.

19. Kanter, op. cit., p. 47.

20. Zablocki, *The Joyful Community*, op. cit., p. 39.

21. Kanter, op. cit., p. 46.

22. Wynne, op. cit., p. 39.

23. Kanter, op. cit., p. 98.

24. Mary Douglas and Aaron Wildavsky, *Risk and Culture: An Essay on the Selection of Technological and Environmental Dangers* (Berkeley: University of California Press, 1982), Chapter 6.

25. Kanter, op. cit., p. 85.

26. Zablocki, *The Joyful Community*, op. cit., p. 172.

27. Linda Boynton, "Religious Orthodoxy, Social Control, and Clothing," unpublished paper presented at the August 1989 meeting of the American Sociological Association, p. 9.

28. Ibid., pp. 12, 16. See also Kai Erikson's *Wayward Puritans* (New York: John Wiley & Sons, 1966) for a description of the unifying functions of deviance in Puritan New England.

29. See Leon Festinger's *When Prophecy Fails* (Minneapolis:

University of Minnesota Press, 1956) for the initial formulation of the concept of cognitive dissonance.

30. Zablocki, *The Joyful Community,* op. cit., p. 185.

31. Albert O. Hirschmann, *Exit, Voice and Loyalty* (Cambridge: Harvard University Press, 1970), Chapter 7.

32. Robert Lifton, *Thought Reform and the Psychology of Totalism* (New York: Norton, 1961), p. 66.

33. Lifton, op. cit., p. 73.

34. Kanter, op. cit., p. 103.

35. Prayer from the rite of religious profession.

36. Veysey, op. cit., p. 273.

37. Zablocki, *Alienation and Charisma,* op. cit., p. 326.

38. Zablocki, *The Joyful Community,* op. cit., p. 281.

39. Kanter, op. cit., Chapter 6.

40. See, for example, Raymond Hostie, *La Vie et Mort des Ordres Religieux* (Paris: Descleé de Brouwer, 1972), and Lawrence Cada, *Shaping the Coming Age of Religious Life* (New York: Seabury Press, 1979). I will be using Cada's categories in the pages which follow.

41. Gerald A. Arbuckle, S.M., *Out of Chaos: Refounding Religious Congregations* (New York: Paulist, 1988).

42. I use "his" advisedly—alone among all the eras of religious life, the mendicant period affected primarily males.

43. Hostie, op. cit., p. 79.

44. Cada, op. cit., p. 30.

45. John W. Padberg, S.J., "Memory, Vision and Structure: Historical Perspectives on the Experience of Religious Life in the Church," pp. 164–78, in Robert J. Daly, S.J. et al., eds., *Religious Life in the U.S. Church: The New Dialogue* (New York: Paulist Press, 1984).

46. Hostie, op. cit., p. 8.

47. Hostie, op. cit., p. 45.

48. Hostie, op. cit., p. 32.

49. Hostie, op. cit., p. 80.

50. Hostie, op. cit., p. 39.

51. Karen Kennelly, C.S.J., "Historical Perspectives on the

Experience of Religious Life in the American Church," pp. 79–97, in Robert J. Daly, S.J. et al., eds., op. cit. See also Mary Ann Donovan, S.C., *Sisterhood as Power: The Past and Passion of Ecclesial Women* (New York: Crossroad, 1989), p. 17.

52. Hostie, op. cit., pp. 40–43.

53. Mary Ewens, O.P., "Women in the Convent," pp. 17–47, in Karen Kennelly, C.S.J., *American Catholic Women: A Historical Exploration* (New York: Macmillan, 1989), p. 33.

54. Hostie, op. cit., p. 43 (translation mine).

55. Hostie, op. cit., p. 158.

56. See Peter L. Berger and Thomas Luckmann, *The Social Construction of Reality: A Treatise on the Sociology of Knowledge* (New York: Doubleday, 1966) for the sociological theory behind this assertion.

57. Zablocki, *Alienation and Charisma*, op. cit., p. 289.

58. Hostie, op. cit., pp. 122–23.

59. Arbuckle, op. cit., p. 69.

60. Rosabeth Kanter and Barry Stein, *Life in Organizations: Workplaces as People Experience Them* (Cambridge: Harvard University Press, 1972), p. 373.

61. Hostie, op. cit., p. 151 (translation mine).

62. Wynne, op. cit., p. 113.

63. Cada, op. cit., p. 75.

64. Marie Augusta Neal, *From Nuns to Sisters: An Expanding Vocation* (Mystic: Twenty-Third Publications, 1990), p. 85.

65. Arbuckle, op. cit., p. 83.

66. Marie Augusta Neal, "Who They Are and What They Do," in Robert Daly et al., eds., op. cit., p. 162.

67. Cada et al., op. cit., p. 48.

68. Neal, op. cit., p. 164.

69. Hostie, op. cit., p. 85.

3. BUREAUCRATIC ORGANIZATION AND RELIGIOUS LIFE

1. "Bureaucracy," pp. 206–217 in the *International Encyclopedia of the Social Sciences*, vol. II (New York: Macmillan, 1968).

2. Ibid.

3. Len Sperry, "Development of Organizations," *Human Development*, vol. 10, #2 (Summer 1989), p. 30.

4. Ibid., p. 31.

5. W.H. Lewis, *Splendid Century* (New York: Sloane, 1954).

6. See Rosabeth Moss Kanter, *Men and Women of the Corporation* (New York: Basic Books, 1977), Chapter 4. See also Georg Simmel, "Subordination under a Principle," pp. 250–253 in Kurt H. Wolff, ed., *The Sociology of Georg Simmel* (New York: Free Press, 1950), who describes an alternative set of values.

7. Charles Perrow. *Organizations: A Critical Essay*, 3rd ed. (New York: Random House, 1986), p. 49.

8. George Ritzer and David Walczak, *Working: Conflict and Change* (Englewood Cliffs: Prentice-Hall, 1986), p. 21.

9. Perrow, op. cit., p. 15.

10. James G. March and Herbert Simon, *Organizations* (New York: John Wiley and Sons, 1958).

11. Weber calls the Catholic Church the oldest bureaucracy in western culture. But the bureaucratic spirit has always been somewhat at odds with the vision of the charismatic leaders who founded religious communities. The history of religious life in chapter 2 could also be read as a struggle over the imposition of bureaucratic forms on religious communities. Religious orders have long been embedded in the larger bureaucratized church structure, and this has "rubbed off" on their own organizational patterns. See H.H. Gerth and C. Wright Mills, *From Max Weber* (New York: Oxford University Press, 1958), pp. 227 and 299.

12. Peter Blau, *The Dynamics of Bureaucracy* (Chicago: University of Chicago Press, 1955), Chapter 3.

13. Robert W. Peterson and Richard A. Schoenherr, "Organizational Status Attainment of Religious Professionals," *Social Forces*, vol. 56, no. 3 (1978), pp. 794–822.

14. Mary Schneider, "The Transformation of American Religious: The Sister Formation Conference as Catalyst for Change, 1954–64," Working Paper Series 17 #1, Cushwa Center for the Study of Catholicism (South Bend: University of Notre Dame, 1986).

15. Marie Augusta Neal, *Catholic Sisters in Transition: From the 1960's to the 1980's* (Wilmington: Michael Glazier, 1984), p. 31.

16. John W. Meyer and Brian Rowan, "Institutionalized Organizations: Formal Structure as Myth and Ceremony," pp. 300–318, in Amitai Etzioni and Edward Lehman, eds., *A Sociological Reader in Complex Organizations*, 2nd ed. (New York: Holt, Rinehart and Winston, 1980).

17. Ibid., p. 304.

18. Gertrude Wemhoff, OSB et al., "Women in Religious Communities." The National Sisters Vocation Conference (1981), pp. 32–33.

19. Max Weber. "Bureaucracy," pp. 24–39, in Frank Fischer and Carmen Sirianni, eds., *Critical Studies in Organization and Bureaucracy* (Philadelphia: Temple University Press, 1984), p. 31.

20. Esther Heffernan, O.P., "Religious Vocations of American Women: Membership in a Socio-Historical Context," unpublished paper, read at the 1989 annual meeting of the Association for the Sociology of Religion, p. 20.

21. Perrow, op. cit., p. 10.

22. Karen M. Kennelley, "Historical Perspectives on the Experience of Religious Life in the American Church," pp. 79–97, in Robert J. Daly, ed., *Religious Life in the U.S. Church: The New Dialogue* (New York: Paulist, 1984), p. 91.

23. Edward A. Wynne, *Traditional Catholic Religious Orders: Living in Community* (New Brunswick: Transaction, 1988), p. 113.

24. I am indebted to Meyer and Rowan, op. cit., for the concept of "decoupling," although they do not use the term in this context.

25. Weber, op. cit., p. 31.

26. Judith Buber Agassi, "Theories of Gender Equality: Lessons from the Israeli Kibbutz," *Gender & Society*, vol. 3, no. 2 (1989), pp. 160–86.

27. March and Simon, op. cit., p. 139.

28. Ibid., p. 143.

29. Perrow, op. cit., pp. 128–31.

30. Perrow, op. cit., pp. 21–22.

31. Kanter, op. cit., pp. 78–82.

32. Larry C. Ingram, "Notes on Pastoral Power in the Congregational Tradition," *Journal for the Scientific Study of Religion*, vol. 19 (1980), pp. 40–48.

33. See, for example, Kathy Ferguson, *The Feminist Case Against Bureaucracy* (Philadelphia: Temple University Press, 1984), and Randall Collins, *The Credential Society* (New York: Academic Press, 1979).

34. Kanter, op. cit., p. 20.

35. Ibid., p. 22.

36. Ibid., p. 25.

37. Patricia Wittberg. "Feminist Consciousness Among American Nuns: Patterns of Ideological Diffusion," *Women's Studies International Forum*, vol. 12, no. 5 (1989), pp. 529–37.

38. Julia Heslin, in a 1983 study of nuns who were principals in New York City parochial schools, found that they had become so at an average age of thirty-four—far younger than the lay women principals. ("In Transition: A Study of Women Religious Administrators in Non-Traditional Roles," Ph.D. Dissertation, Fordham University.)

39. Collins, op. cit.

40. William Ouchi, *Theory Z: How American Business Can Meet the Japanese Challenge* (Reading: Addison Wesley, 1981).

4. THE ASSOCIATIONAL MODEL
AND RELIGIOUS LIFE

1. Helen Rose Fuchs Ebaugh. *Becoming an Ex: The Process of Role Exit* (Chicago: University of Chicago Press, 1988), p. 44.
2. Patricia Wittberg. "Transformations in Religious Commitment," *Review for Religious*, vol. 44, #2 (1985), pp. 161–70.
3. Douglas B. McGaw. "Commitment and Religious Community: A Comparison of a Charismatic and a Mainline Congregation," *Journal for the Scientific Study of Religion*, vol. 18, no. 2 (1979), pp. 146–63.
4. Mark Granovetter. "The Strength of Weak Ties," *American Journal of Sociology*, vol. 78, no. 6 (1973), p. 1361.
5. An entire literature exists on this subject. Among the classics are Ferdinand Toennies' *Community and Society* (New York: Harper & Row, 1963), Louis Wirth's "Urbanism as a Way of Life," *American Journal of Sociology*, vol. 44, no. 1, pp. 1–24, and Georg Simmel's "The Metropolis and Mental Life," in Kurt Wolff, ed., *The Sociology of Georg Simmel* (New York: Free Press, 1950), pp. 409–424.
6. Wirth, op. cit., p. 17.
7. See Granovetter, 1973, op. cit. I will be following Granovetter's analysis closely in the pages that follow.
8. Granovetter, 1973, op. cit., pp. 1363–64.
9. Ibid., p. 1366.
10. Stanley Milgram. "The Small World Problem," *Psychology Today* (May 1967), pp. 62–67. See also Jeffrey Travers and Stanley Milgram, "An Experimental Study of the 'Small World,'" *Sociometry*, vol. 32 (December 1969) pp. 425–43.
11. Granovetter, op. cit., p. 1368.
12. Ibid., p. 1370.
13. Mark Granovetter. "The Strength of Weak Ties: A Network Theory Revisited," pp. 105–130, in Peter V. Marsden and Nan Lin, eds., *Social Structure and Network Theory* (Berkeley: Sage, 1982). See also Carol Stack, *All Our Kin* (New York: Harper and Row, 1974).

14. Granovetter, 1982, op. cit., p. 166.

15. Granovetter, 1973, op. cit., p. 1370.

16. Ibid., p. 1365.

17. Jessica Lipnack and Jeffrey Stamps, *Networking: The First Report and Directory* (New York: Doubleday, 1982).

18. Herbert Gans, *The Urban Villagers* (New York: Free Press, 1962).

19. Granovetter, 1982, op. cit., p. 106.

20. Granovetter, 1973, op. cit., p. 1375.

21. John D. McCarthy and Mayer N. Zald, "Resource Mobilization and Social Movements: A Partial Theory," *American Journal of Sociology*, vol. 82, no. 6 (1977), pp. 1212–41.

22. J. Miller McPherson and Lynn Smith-Lovin, "Women and Weak Ties: Differences by Sex in the Size of Voluntary Organizations," *American Journal of Sociology*, vol. 87, no. 4 (1982), pp. 883–904.

23. Ibid., p. 888.

24. Edward Shils. *Center and Periphery* (Chicago: University of Chicago Press, 1979).

25. McPherson and Smith-Lovin, op. cit., p. 901.

26. Ibid., p. 901.

27. Granovetter, 1973, op. cit., p. 1373.

28. At the American Sociological Association conference in Chicago in 1987, I had breakfast with one of the foremost sociologists of gender stratification in the country, one of whose professional colleagues had left a religious community in the early 1970s. She expressed her astonishment—and envy—at the range of her colleague's contacts, even fifteen years after having left the convent. I assured her that most nuns had similarly wide-ranging connections, even if they were not aware of them and never used them.

29. Margaret S. Thompson's article, "Discovering Foremothers: Sisters, Society, and the American Catholic Experience," *U.S. Catholic Historian*, vol. 5, nos. 3 & 4 (1986), p. 288, documents how Mother Cabrini used her network to advise fellow religious superiors on ways to attain pontifical status over their local bishop's opposition.

30. Mary Ewens, O.P., "Women in the Convent." pp. 17–47, in Karen Kennelly, C.S.J., ed., *American Catholic Women: A Historical Exploration* (New York: Macmillan, 1989), p. 34.

31. Granovetter, 1982, op. cit., pp. 24–25.

32. Twosomes are more likely—see Patricia Wittberg, "Dyads and Triads: The Sociological Implications of Small-Group Living Arrangements," *Review for Religious*, vol. 49, no. 1 (1990), pp. 43–51.

33. Patricia Wittberg, "Roman Catholic Religious Orders of Women in the United States: The Implications of Structural Change," unpublished paper read at the October 1989 meeting of the Society for the Scientific Study of Religion.

34. Robert E. Moran, C.S.P., *Death and Rebirth: A Case Study of Reform Efforts of a Roman Catholic Sisterhood*, Ph.D dissertation, University of California, Santa Barbara, 1972.

35. Ibid., p. 232.

36. Donna Markham, O.P., "The Decline of Vocations in the United States," *New Catholic World*, vol. 231, no. 1381 (Jan/Feb. 1988).

37. Erving Goffman, *The Presentation of Self in Everyday Life* (New York: Doubleday, 1959), pp. 86, 92.

38. Moran, op. cit., p. 225.

39. The Grail appears to follow this model. Another example might be the associate programs emerging in many congregations.

40. Gerald Arbuckle, S.M., "The Marginalization of Social Scientists Within the Church," *Human Development*, vol. 10, no. 2 (1989), pp. 16–21.

41. Benjamin Zablocki, *Alienation and Charisma* (New York: Free Press, 1980), p. 289; Rosabeth Moss Kanter, *Commitment and Community* (Cambridge: Harvard University Press, 1972), p. 77.

42. See, for example, Ruth P. Liebowitz, "Virgins in the Service of Christ: The Dispute Over the Active Apostolate of Women During the Counter-Reformation," in Rosemary Ruether and Eleanor McLaughlin, eds., *Women of Spirit* (New York: Simon and Schuster, 1979).

5. RECRUITING AND RETAINING GROUP MEMBERS

1. Charles Perrow. *Complex Organizations: A Critical Essay*, 3rd ed. (New York: Random House, 1986), pp. 159–64.

2. Kristen Wenzel, O.S.U., "The Impact of Religiousness on Retirement Expectations Among Women Religious in the U.S.," unpublished paper presented at the 1990 meeting of the Eastern Sociological Society, Boston, p. 1. See also Elizabeth Kolmer, *Religious Women in the U.S.* (Wilmington: Michael Glazier, 1984), pp. 16, 41, and Marie Augusta Neal, *Catholic Sisters in Transition: From the 1960's to the 1980's* (Wilmington: Michael Glazier, 1984), pp. 18–19.

3. "Counting Jesuit Losses," *Religion Watch*, vol. 4, #3 (January 1989), p. 4.

4. *Pro Mundi Vita*, "New Beginnings," Bulletin 92 (Spring 1983), p. 7.

5. John M. Staudenmaier, S.J., "Adult Commitment at Century's End: Some Technological Influences," pp. 116–137, in Laurie Felknor, ed., *The Crisis in Religious Vocations: An Inside View* (New York: Paulist Press, 1989), p. 117.

6. Esther Heffernan, O.P., "Religious Vocations of American Women: Membership in a Socio-Historical Context," paper presented at the August 1989 meeting of the Association for the Sociology of Religion, San Francisco, p. 16.

7. Gerald Arbuckle, S.M., *Out of Chaos: Refounding Religious Congregations* (New York: Paulist Press, 1988), pp. 42–43. See also Donna Markham, O.P., "The Decline of Vocations in the U.S.," pp. 181–196, in Felknor, ed., op. cit.

8. Thomas Robbins, *Cults, Converts and Charisma: The Sociology of New Religious Movements* (Berkeley: Sage, 1988), p. 87.

9. Ibid.

10. John Lofland, *Doomsday Cult* (Englewood Cliffs: Prentice-Hall, 1966).

11. Karl Mannheim, *Essays on the Sociology of Knowledge* (New York: Oxford University Press, 1952), pp. 276–320.

12. Mary Ewens, O.P., "Women in the Convent," pp. 17–47,

in Karen Kennelly, C.S.J., ed., *American Catholic Women: A Historical Exploration* (New York: Macmillan, 1989), p. 37.

13. Patricia Wittberg, S.C., "The Problem of Generations in Religious Life," *Review for Religious,* vol. 47, no. 6 (November-December 1988), p. 902.

14. Ibid., p. 903.

15. Rosabeth Moss Kanter, *Commitment and Community: Communes and Utopias in Sociological Perspective* (Cambridge: Harvard University Press, 1972), p. 146.

16. Robbins, op. cit., p. 100.

17. Dean Hoge et al., "Changing Age Distribution and Theological Attitudes of Catholic Priests: 1970–1985," *Sociological Analysis,* vol. 40:3 (1988), p. 272.

18. Carroll Stuhlmueller, C.P., "Biblical Observations on the Decline of Vocation to Religious Life," pp. 152–164, in Felknor, ed., op. cit., p. 161.

19. Richard A. Schoenherr and Annemette Sorensen, "Social Change in Religious Organizations: Consequences of Clergy Decline in the U.S.," *Sociological Analysis,* vol. 43:1 (1982), p. 45.

20. Patricia Wittberg, S.C., "Outward Orientation in Declining Organizations: Reflections on the LCWR Documents," pp. 89–105, in Nadine Foley, ed., *Claiming Our Truth: Reflections on Identity by U.S. Women Religious* (Washington, DC: LCWR, 1988).

21. Carroll Stuhlmueller, C.P., op. cit., p. 153.

22. J. Miller McPherson and Lynn Smith-Lovin, "Women and Weak Ties: Differences by Sex in the Size of Voluntary Organizations," *American Journal of Sociology,* vol. 87:4 (1982), p. 899.

23. Mary Ann Donovan, S.C., "A More Limited Witness: An Historical Theologian Looks at the Signposts," pp. 84–98, in Felknor, ed., op. cit., pp. 91–92. See also Mary Ewens, *Women in the Convent,* op. cit., p. 42.

24. James Hennessey, S.J., "A Look at the Institution Itself," pp. 32–39, in Felknor, ed., op. cit., p. 37.

25. Mary Ann Donovan, op. cit., p. 94.

26. Donna Markham, O.P., op. cit., pp. 184–85.

27. Archdiocese of Newark, Vocations Office, "Recommendations Given by 3000 High School Youth To Encourage Vocations to Religious Life," unpublished paper, 1987.

28. Benjamin Zablocki, *Alienation and Charisma: A Study of Contemporary American Communes* (New York: Free Press, 1980), p. 289.

29. Robbins, op. cit., p. 83.

30. National Opinion Research Center, *The Catholic Priest in the U.S.: Sociological Investigations* (Washington, D.C.: U.S. Catholic Conference, 1972), pp. 270–71.

31. Daniel P. O'Neill, "St. Paul's Priests, 1850–1930: Recruitment, Ethnicity and Americanization," pp. 70–77, in Dolores Liptak, ed., *A Church of Many Cultures* (New York: Garland, 1988), p. 76.

32. Hennessey, op. cit., p. 37.

33. Archdiocese of Newark, Vocations Office, unpublished summary letter to religious congregations, 1988.

34. Lofland, op. cit.

35. Joseph H. Fichter, S.J., "Vanishing Church Professionals," pp. 99–118, in Felknor, op. cit., p. 105.

36. John W. Padburg, S.J., "The Contexts of Comings and Goings," pp. 19–31, in Felknor, op. cit., pp. 26–27.

37. Markham, op. cit., p. 184.

38. Robbins, op. cit., p. 73.

39. Henry B. Leonard, "Ethnic Tension, Episcopal Leadership and the Emergence of the Twentieth Century American Catholic Church," pp. 196–214, in Liptak, op. cit.

40. Mary Ann Donovan, S.C., *Sisterhood as Power: The Past and Passion of Ecclesial Women.* (New York: Crossroad, 1989), p. 53.

41. Mary Ewens, O.P., "The Vocation Decline of Women Religious: Some Historical Perspectives," pp. 165–80, in Felknor, op. cit., pp. 167–76.

42. Raymond Hostie, *La Vie et Mort des Ordres Religieux* (Paris: Descleé de Brouwer, 1972), pp. 284–85.

43. Donald Senior, C.P., "A Biblical Perspective on Why They Left," pp. 141–151, in Felknor, op. cit., pp. 146–47.

44. Robert Bellah et al., *Habits of the Heart* (New York: Harper and Row, 1985), pp. 46–47.

45. Edward A. Wynne, *Traditional Catholic Religious Orders: Living in Community* (New Brunswick: Transaction, 1988), pp. 68–69.

46. It may occur to the reader at this point that, in Chapter 1, I had stated that America is an exceptionally fertile ground for the development of intentional communities. How can this be, if our cultural values are so opposed to them? Kai Erikson, in a study of a town devastated by floods—*Everything in Its Path* (New York: Simon and Schuster, 1976), pp. 81–93—makes the interesting observation that cultures have "fault lines" of polarization between two opposing values. Whereas one pole is usually manifested (in this case, the values Senior has listed), in times of stress individuals may slide along the continuum of their culture's "fault line" all the way to the opposite extreme.

47. George Gallup, Jr. and Jim Castelli, *The American Catholic People: Their Beliefs, Practices and Values* (New York: Doubleday, 1987), p. 2.

48. Marie Augusta Neal. *From Nuns to Sisters: An Expanding Vocation* (Mystic: Twenty-Third Publications, 1990), p. 32.

49. Ewens, "The Vocation Decline," op. cit., p. 179.

50. Dean Hoge, *The Future of Catholic Leadership: Responses to the Priest Shortage* (Kansas City: Sheed and Ward, 1987), p. 134. See also Archdiocese of Newark, op. cit.

51. L. Miller Bernal, "Sex and Dating: College Men's and Women's Attitudes," Paper presented at the October 1986 meeting of the New York State Sociological Association.

52. Jay P. Dolan, "Immigrants in the City: New York's Irish and German Catholics," in Brian C. Mitchell, ed., *Building the American Catholic City* (New York: Garland, 1988), pp. 49–51. See also Kathleen Gavigan, "The Rise and Fall of Parish Cohesiveness in Philadelphia," in the same anthology, pp. 117–24.

53. Pontifical Commission on Religious Life, "U.S. Religious Life and the Decline of Vocations," *Origins*, vol. 16, no. 25 (December 4, 1986), p. 469.

54. Stephen Hart, "Privatization in American Religion and Society," *Sociological Analysis,* vol. 47, no. 4 (Winter 1987).

55. Wittberg, *The Problem of Generations,* op. cit., p. 911.

56. John Deedy, "The Catechism Crisis: Can Catholics Pass Religion 101?" *U.S. Catholic* (August 1984), pp. 20–24. See also Matt Scheiber, "Mass Confusion on a Catholic Campus," in the same issue.

57. Hoge, op. cit., p. 121.

58. Alan Riding, "Conservative Catholic Group Casts Off Its Cloak," *New York Times,* October 25, 1989. See also "Opus Dei Gaining Influence in Brazil," *Religion Watch,* vol. 4, #11 (October 1989), p. 8.

59. The National Sisters Vocation Conference found that vocation offices did increase vocations slightly; Markham (in Felknor, op. cit., p. 193) found no effect.

60. "Opus Dei Gaining Influence in Brazil," *Religion Watch,* vol. 4, #11 (October 1989), p. 8.

61. Moises Sandoval. "My House Is Your House," *Maryknoll Magazine,* vol. 83, #10 (October 1989), pp. 49–50. See also M. Sandoval, "Hispanic Vocations: A Bountiful Harvest?" *Maryknoll Magazine,* vol. 82, #10 (October 1988), pp. 22–26.

62. "Counting Jesuit Losses," *Religion Watch,* vol. 4, #3 (January 1989), p. 4.

63. Roger Finke and Rodney Stark. "How the Upstart Sects Won America: 1776–1850," *Journal for the Scientific Study of Religion,* vol. 28, #1 (March 1989), pp. 27–44.

64. Edmundo Rodriguez, S.J., "Realities for Hispanics," *Company,* vol. 6, no. 1 (Fall 1989), p. 9.

65. Joseph Fichter (op. cit., p. 106) has found that abuses of authority were the most important reason for leaving the priesthood among the priests he surveyed. And the diocesan priesthood is a relatively bureaucratized area—abuses of authority would be even more likely in more communitarian groups.

6. INSTITUTIONALIZED MINISTRIES AND RELIGIOUS LIFE

1. The sociological definition of "institution" refers to a pattern of roles and values which have sprung up in a society to meet a social need. In sociology, therefore, the family, religion, the educational system as a whole, medicine and even sports would be examples of institutions. See Ian Robertson, *Sociology*, 3rd ed. (New York: Worth, 1987), pp. 93–94, or any college introductory sociology text. However there is also a tradition in sociology that uses "institution" as I am using it here. This is the so-called institutional school of research in the sociology of formal organizations. See Charles Perrow, *Complex Organizations: A Critical Essay*, 3rd ed. (New York: Random House, 1986, chapter 5) for a summary of this literature.

2. John W. Meyer and Brian Rowan. "Institutionalized Organizations: Formal Structure as Myth and Ceremony," pp. 300–18, in Amitai Etzioni and Edward Lehman, eds., *A Sociological Reader in Complex Organizations*, 2nd ed. (New York: Holt, Rinehart and Winston, 1980).

3. James Hennesey, S.J., "A Look at the Institution Itself," in Laurie Felknor, ed., *The Crisis in Religious Vocations* (New York: Paulist, 1989).

4. Rosemary Pringle, "Bureaucracy, Rationality and Sexuality: The Case of Secretaries," pp. 158–77, in Jeff Hearn et al., eds., *The Sexuality of Organization* (Newbury Park: Sage, 1989), p. 161.

5. Wilfred Brown, quoted in Perrow, op. cit., pp. 21–22.

6. Marshall W. Meyer and Lynne G. Zucker. *Permanently Failing Organizations* (Newbury Park: Sage Publications, 1989), p. 19.

7. Ibid., p. 23.

8. Ibid., pp. 35–38. I am relying heavily on Meyer and Zucker for this summary.

9. Ibid., p. 36.

10. Ibid., p. 81.

11. Ibid., pp. 37–38.

12. Ibid., p. 83.

13. Andrew Greeley, William McCready and K. McCourt, *Catholic Schools in a Declining Church* (Kansas City: Sheed and Ward, 1976), p. 39.

14. Mary E. Mulcahy, "Financial Crisis in the Parochial Schools," unpublished paper, 1989, Department of Sociology, Anthropology and Social Work, Illinois State University.

15. Meyer and Zucker, op. cit., p. 31.

16. Ibid., p. 24.

17. Robert Perrucci and Harry R. Potter, eds., *Networks of Power* (New York: Aldine de Gruyter, 1989), Introduction, p. 8.

18. Mary Ewens, "The Leadership of Nuns in Immigrant Catholicism," pp. 101–49, in Rosemary Ruether and R.S. Keller, eds., *Women and Religion in America*, vol. 1 (New York: Harper and Row, 1981), p. 107.

19. J. Kenneth Benson, "The Inter-Organizational Network as a Political Economy," pp. 349–68, in Etzioni and Lehman, op. cit.

20. James G. March and Herbert Simon, *Organizations* (New York: John Wiley and Sons, 1958).

21. Alvin Gouldner, *Patterns of Industrial Bureaucracy* (New York: Free Press, 1954).

22. This is not the same as the current movement whereby congregations sponsoring health care institutions join forces to create umbrella corporations. While this process may lead to a congregation's becoming the nominal sponsor of a whole new set of hospitals or nursing facilities, it is not the same as the institutionalization of a new work.

7. THE SEED

1. Gerald Arbuckle, S.M., *Out of Chaos: Refounding Religious Congregations* (New York: Paulist Press, 1988), p. 83.

2. Benjamin Zablocki. *Alienation and Charisma: A Study of Contemporary American Communes* (New York: Free Press, 1980), p. 289.

3. Rosabeth M. Kanter and Barry Stein, "Organizational Death Watch," in Rosabeth Moss Kanter and Barry Stein, eds., *Life in Organizations: Workplaces as People Experience Them* (Cambridge: Harvard University Press, 1972), pp. 373–87.

4. Mary Jo Leddy: "Beyond the Liberal Model," in *The Way*, Supplement #65, *Religious Life in Transition* (Summer 1989), p. 46.

5. Ibid., p. 45.

6. It is these small groups that have come to be called "intentional communities" in some religious congregations. Most, however, do not make the kinds of wide-ranging demands upon their members that intentional communities as sociologically defined would make. They can more profitably be seen as small, creative amalgamations of some communitarian characteristics within the larger, more associational or bureaucratic, congregation.

7. *Pro Mundi Vita*, "New Beginnings: Religious Life Evolves," Bulletin 92 (Spring 1983).

8. Patricia Wittberg. "Dyads and Triads: The Sociological Implications of Small-Group Living Arrangements," *Review for Religious*, vol. 49, no. 1 (January-February 1990), pp. 43–51.

9. Raymond Hostie, *La Vie et Mort Des Ordres Religieux* (Paris: Descleé De Brouwer, 1972), p. 79.

10. Ibid., p. 32.

11. Joan Chittister, O.S.B., *Women, Ministry and the Church* (New York: Paulist Press, 1983), p. 30.

12. John M Staudenmaier, S.J., "Adult Commitment at Century's End," in Laurie Felknor, ed., *The Crisis in Religious Vocations* (New York: Paulist Press, 1989), p. 117.

13. *Pro Mundi Vita*, op. cit., pp. 12–22. See also M. Basil Pennington, "Temporary Monasticism," *America* (April 9, 1988), pp. 380–81.

14. Marie Augusta Neal, S.N.D., *From Nuns to Sisters: An*

Expanding Vocation (Mystic: Twenty-Third Publications, 1990), p. 15.

15. Georg Simmel, "The Secret Society," in Kurt H. Wolff, ed., *The Sociology of Georg Simmel* (New York: Free Press, 1950), p. 360.

16. Robert N. Bellah et al., *Habits of the Heart* (New York: Harper and Row, 1985), p. 48.

17. Matt Scheiber, "Mass Confusion on a Catholic Campus," *U.S. Catholic* (August 1984), pp. 25–27. John Deedy, "The Catechism Crisis: Can Catholics Pass Religion 101?" *U.S. Catholic* (August 1984), pp. 20–24. E. Nancy McAuley and Moira Mathieson, *Faith Without Form: Beliefs of Catholic Youth* (Kansas City: Sheed and Ward, 1986).

18. Joan Fee et al., *Young Catholics in the United States and Canada: A Report to the Knights of Columbus* (Los Angeles: Sadlier, 1981), p. 95.

19. Ibid., p. 25.

20. Ibid., pp. 96–97.

21. Edmundo Rodriguez, S.J., "Realities for Hispanics," *Company* (Fall 1988), pp. 9–10.

22. *Pro Mundi Vita,* op. cit., p. 10.

23. Clyde Haberman, "A Sympathetic Pope Visits Some of Africa's Poorest," *New York Times,* January 29, 1990, p. A13.

24. See, for example, Paula J. Caplan, "Anti-Feminist Women," *International Journal of Women's Studies,* vol. 8 (1985), pp. 351–54; Iva E. Deutchman and Sandra Prince-Embry, "Political Ideology of Pro- and Anti-ERA Women," *Women and Politics,* vol. 2 (1982), pp. 39–55; Denise Kulp, "Inside Right-Wing Women's Culture," *Off Our Backs,* vol. 15 (May 1985), pp. 16–17; Susan D. Rose, "Women Warriors: The Negotiation of Gender in a Charismatic Congregation," *Sociological Analysis,* vol. 48 (1987), pp. 245–58; Robyn Rowland, "Women Who Do and Women Who Don't Join the Women's Movement," *Women's Studies International Forum,* vol. 8 (1985), pp. 249–54.

25. Margaret Gannon, I.H.M., "A World Church and Chris-

tian Feminism," pp. 121–39, in Nadine Foley, O.P., ed., *Claiming Our Truth: Reflections on Identity by U.S. Women Religious* (Washington: Leadership Conference of Women Religious, 1988), especially pp. 133–36.

26. Bellah et al., op. cit., p. 65.

27. Ibid., p. 81.

28. Patricia Wittberg, S.C., "Transformations in Religious Commitment," *Review for Religious*, vol. 44, no. 2 (1985). See also a summary of this article in chapter 2.

29. *Pro Mundi Vita*, op. cit.

30. M. Grace Swift, O.S.U., "The White-Robed Citadins of Paris," *Review for Religious*, vol. 40, no. 3 (May/June 1981), pp. 338–44.

31. *Pro Mundi Vita*, op. cit., p. 6.

32. Hostie, op. cit., p. 122.

33. *Pro Mundi Vita*, op. cit., pp. 22–23.

34. Paula Gonzalez, S.C., "Communication, Technology and Ecology: A Response to John M. Staudenmaier," in James McDonnell and Frances Trampiets, S.C., eds., *Communicating Faith in a Technological Age* (London: St. Paul Publications, 1989).

35. I am indebted for this example to Esther Heffernan, O.P.

36. Esther Heffernan, O.P. personal communication.

37. *Pro Mundi Vita*, op. cit., p. 14.

38. Pat Brockman, O.S.U. "New Jerusalem—A Story of Community," *LCWR Occasional Papers*, vol. 16, no. 3 (October 1989), pp. 13–14.

Index